Table of Contents

Preface

The inspiration for this book came from the many students I have taught in quilt shops and guilds throughout Southern California. Students in every class and lecture asked for patterns or a book. Since there was no single book I could refer them to, I decided to write my own. I hope to share the joy of making fast and easy quilts with stencils, paint, pens, and embellishments.

Whatever you do, please don't be intimidated by the painting in this book. The instructions are so easy—anyone, even the "unartistic," can make beautiful stenciled quilts. I myself have had no formal artistic training. I have no special skills, just the tricks and secrets I will share with you in this book.

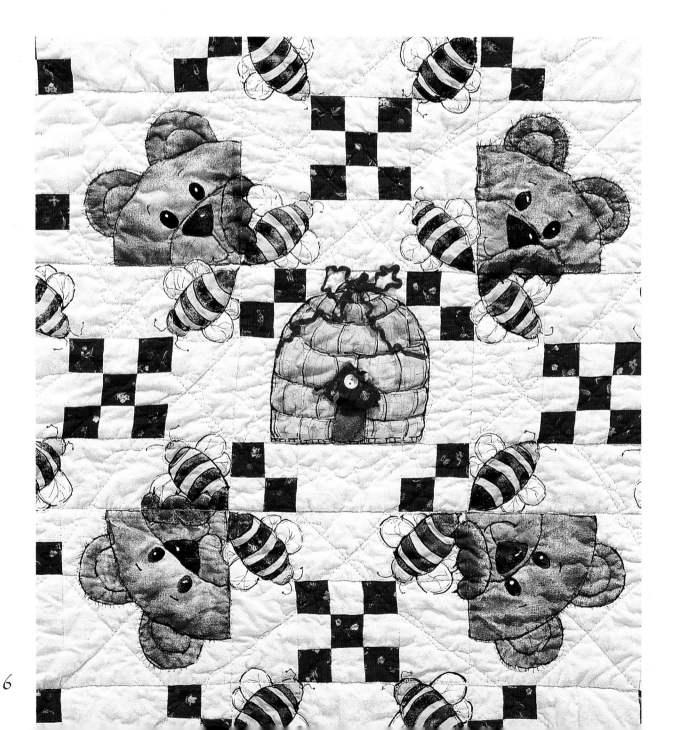

Introduction

Stenciling is fast, fun, and easy, and the projects in this book are almost foolproof. If you can cut paper, dab paint, scribble a crooked line, sew a seam, and stitch on a button, then you can make any one of the small quilts and pillow tops. With a bit more quiltmaking know-how, you can whip up a stunning wall-size quilt.

To stencil, you need a stencil, a surface to stencil, paint, and a tool for applying paint. This book uses freezer paper for the stencil, fabric for the stencil surface, acrylic craft paint, and sponges to apply the paint. Since most of us have fabric, some type of paint, sponges, and maybe even freezer paper already at hand, it is easy to begin. Use what you have, then if you like the process, buy the materials listed in the supply list. I want this to be simple and fun.

Make a Quilt As You Learn

Each chapter teaches you a technique, then lets you try that technique on a sample project. By the time you have learned to stencil, scribble, stitch, and embellish, you will have completed this adorable miniature House quilt. Let's start the process now!

Make this fast and easy miniature House quilt as you learn.

Can You Cut Paper?
Then You Can Make a Stencil!

What Is a Stencil?

A stencil is a piece of paper or other material with holes cut out in a design. Paint or ink is applied through the holes to the surface beneath to form the design. Since the background is covered by the uncut area around the design, stenciling is a simple and almost foolproof craft.

What makes these stencils different? The purchased stenciled design (left) has gaps where bridges hold the stencil together. I prefer the stenciled design on the right, without bridge sections—it's mine, of course!

Stencil Terms Defined

Every technique has its own language. To effectively make and use stencils, it helps to know what the different parts are called. Below is a sketch of a stencil with the parts labeled.

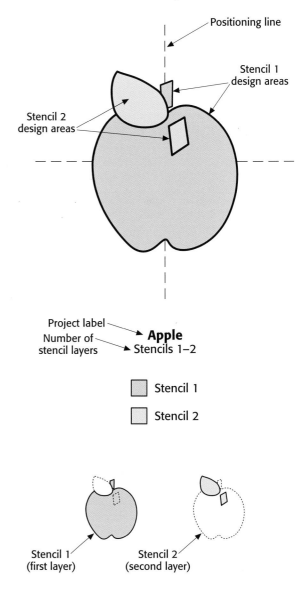

Positioning lines: dashed lines that allow you to correctly position the stencil on the background fabric.

Project label: the name of the design or project.

Stencil design area: designates the hole to be cut in the paper. It is the area you remove to make the stencil.

Stencil (noun): the whole shebang. It is a piece of freezer paper with the design area cut out, ready to fuse and paint.

Stencil (verb): to dab the paint in the hole or stencil design area.

Stenciler: YOU, after you use this book!

Stencil Cutting

Supplies

- Freezer paper: I buy the Reynolds brand at the grocery store. If you can't find it, call Reynolds at (804) 281-4630.
- Pencil
- Cuticle scissors or craft knife
- Rotary cutter, acrylic ruler, and cutting mat (optional)

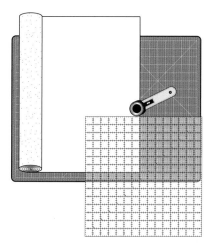

- Pattern: To begin with, use the simple designs in this book. After you have used a few multilayered stencils, try designing your own. Stencils can be

made from almost anything. Coloring books, iron-on transfer designs, appliqué patterns, and tole designs are all great sources.

Directions

1. Most of the designs in this book are stenciled in layers. The stencil patterns are color-coded so you can see which design areas to cut for a given stencil. Determine how many stencils you need to cut for your design (in the case of our sample apple, 2). For each stencil, cut a piece of freezer paper large enough to cover the pattern plus 2" all around. (I use a dull rotary cutter, mat, and ruler).

2. Center the freezer paper on top of the pattern with the dull side up.

3. With a pencil, trace the entire design. Be sure to include the dashed positioning lines. Repeat for any subsequent stencils; for example, the apple calls for 2 stencils, so you would need to make 2 tracings.

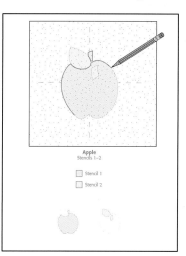

Apple
Stencils 1–2

Stencil 1
Stencil 2

4. Write the pattern name on each tracing, and the stencil number (i.e., stencil #1, stencil #2).

5. To cut out the design areas, use cuticle scissors or a craft knife. First poke a hole in the center of the design area. Do not cut from the outside edge of the paper into the traced area. Cut inside the design only, leaving the surrounding area uncut. In this example, you would cut out the pink shapes for stencil #1 and the apricot shapes for #2.

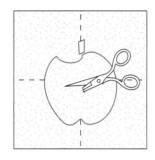

Poke hole.

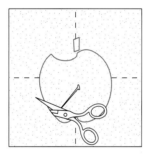

Cut along traced line.

NOTE: Freezer-paper stencils can be used up to six times. Simply peel off and re-fuse. This means that unless you need to repeat a design more than six times, one of each stencil layer is enough.

Little House Project

Gather the supplies listed on page 9.

Directions

1. Cut a piece of freezer paper large enough to cover the Little House plus 2" all around.

2. Lay the freezer paper on top of the house pattern, with the dull side of the freezer paper facing up. Make sure the house is centered on the paper and the bottom of the house is straight.

3. With a pencil, trace the entire design and the dashed positioning lines. Write the pattern name and stencil number on the freezer paper as well (i.e., Little House stencil #1).

4. Use cuticle scissors or a craft knife to cut out the pink areas in the small diagram (house and chimney).

5. Repeat for stencil #2, removing just the areas indicated in the small diagram of stencil #2 (apricot).

You have made a stencil and are ready to start dabbing paint.

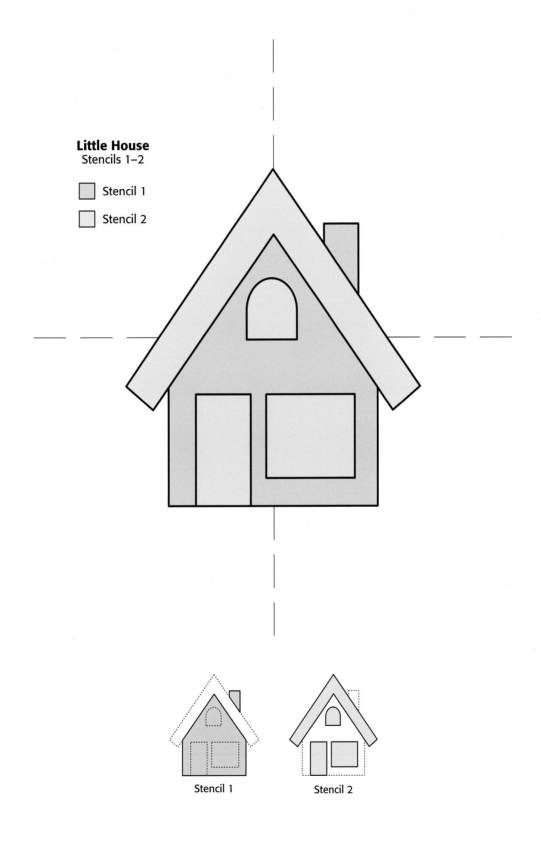

Little House
Stencils 1–2

Stencil 1

Stencil 2

Stencil 1

Stencil 2

Can You Dab Paint?
Then You Can Stencil!

Some of the supplies and methods I use are a bit different from traditional stenciling. I have no art background and artists intimidate me, but I have learned to do a lot of "artistic" things through trial and error. This chapter explains the unusual methods and materials I have discovered. I promise you will be stenciling that house soon.

Fabric Choices

Background

Don't feel limited to plain fabrics for your stencil backgrounds. I use lots of different fabrics to keep the backgrounds interesting. Here are some fabrics I like to use:

Small-scale prints, checks, stripes, and plaids are perfect for stencil backgrounds. Check the back of your print. Is it more subtle, less defined on the back? You bought both sides of the fabric—go ahead and use both sides!

Printed tone-on-tone muslin is wonderful to stencil. The print appears in the paint as a secondary design. I love when this happens.

Solids in any color are also good choices. Start with light-colored solid backgrounds until you get confident, but be sure to avoid bright white backgrounds if you plan to use white paint.

Borders

The border on a little stenciled quilt is the perfect place to use those fat quarters and bits of fabric you bought but haven't used. Almost anything goes. If you like the way your design looks with a big splashy floral, then use it. If you like quieter, more polite borders, by all means use those.

Backing

Always use 100% cotton for backings. I either choose a fabric that relates to the stencil, or I use muslin so I can write a message on the back.

Batting

I use Hobbs Heirloom, Warm & Natural, Fairfield cotton, Pellon Fleece, or Thermolam Plus. Do not use polyester batting. It makes the quilt too fat and does not hold the weight of embellishments well.

Paint

I use regular acrylic craft paint for almost all of my fabric stenciling—the kind found in the bottle at the fabric or crafts store. My favorites are Delta Ceramcoat, Liquitex Acrylic (both tube and bottle), and DecoArt's Americana and Plaid Apple Barrel. Any acrylic craft paint or fabric paint can be used to stencil.

When I teach or lecture, someone always asks me, "What about washing?" Most students are surprised to hear I use craft paint even on

Acrylic craft paints

projects I plan to wash. I hand wash with a mild soap, and the paint holds up remarkably well. The only exception is when the project is to be machine washed frequently with the regular laundry. In that case, I recommend fabric paint or dye.

Dry cleaning is not recommended by any of the paint or dye manufacturers. Dry-cleaning solvents can destroy the paints. Embellishments are a problem, too; most dry cleaners don't want to deal with them.

Stencil Brushes

When I began stenciling, I was flabbergasted to learn I needed to buy a brush for every color I used. This can get expensive, so my students and I have devised some simple ways to cut the expense and make it easier to get started.

Vicki's Brush Rule Breakers

• You can use a brush for more than one color. After you finish stenciling with one color, wash the brush. Using paper towels or an absorbent cloth, dry the brush thoroughly so no water is left in the bristles. Once the bristles are very, very dry to the touch, you may reuse the brush.

• Any stiff-bristled brush can be used to dab paint in the smaller openings of a stencil. Of course, stencil brushes are still easiest for the larger openings.

Stencil brushes

• Sponge brushes, sponges, fabric bundles, eye-makeup applicators, even Q-tips are all good alternatives to brushes. Match the painting tool to the size of the opening to be stenciled.

For fabric stenciling, I recommend buying brush sizes ¼", ⅜", and ½" to start with. Use a good brush cleaner or shampoo with conditioner to wash the brushes. I use Masters Brush Cleaner. It even cleans brushes full of dried-out paint.

Sponges

Sponges are a cheap and easy substitute for brushes when you are stenciling. All of the smaller examples were done with sponges instead of brushes. Use one for each color of paint, then toss it when you finish the project. Different sponges give different results. Sponges with large, open surfaces leave a rough, open texture in the paint. This texture is good for snow, hair, and bushes.

Triangular cosmetic sponges are my favorite. These wedges come in large bags at drugstores, discount stores, and grocery stores and do not need any preparation, though you can cut them down for small openings.

Large rectangular sponges can be cut to any size with household scissors. I cut them to the size of the stencil opening I need to paint. A good size for stenciling the projects in this book is 1" x 2". Try different sizes, then use what feels most comfortable.

Stencil sponges: yellow car-washing sponge, white makeup wedges, and green kitchen sponge

Stencil Basics: How to Dab

Whether you prefer to stencil with a sponge or a brush, the technique is basically the same. For the projects in this book, I recommend using sponges. If you'd like to try stenciling with a brush, however, proceed with the sponging directions that follow, substituting a dry brush for the sponge. Hold the brush in an upright position, and remember to blot excess paint on a paper towel.

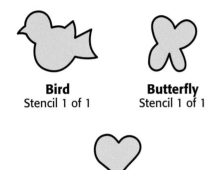

Bird
Stencil 1 of 1

Butterfly
Stencil 1 of 1

Heart
Stencil 1 of 1

NOTE: If you accidentally spatter paint on your project, don't despair! Make stray spots look intentional by stenciling over them. Use the small, cheery shapes above or come up with some of your own.

SPONGE STENCILING

Supplies

- Iron and ironing board
- Freezer-paper stencils
- Acrylic craft paint
- Paper plate
- Paper towels
- Sponges
- White tissue paper or muslin for press cloth

Directions

1. Cut a piece of fabric the size indicated in the project directions.
2. Fold the fabric in half and in half again and crease. Unfold.
3. Set the iron on "cotton" with no steam. Place the fabric right side up on the ironing board. Lay stencil #1 on it, dull side up, matching the positioning lines on the stencil to the creases on the fabric.

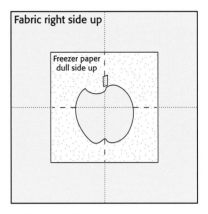

Place positioning lines at creases.

4. Iron the stencil to the fabric. This takes about 30 seconds. Test the edges from time to time and stop when they are fused.
5. Prepare to paint: Place a piece of freezer paper on your work surface to protect it. Pour a tablespoon of the desired paint color on the paper plate. Fold a piece of paper towel in half and put next to the paper plate.
6. Grasp a dry sponge on opposite sides with your thumb and index finger so the large surface is down. The exposed area at the bottom of the sponge will be your painting surface.

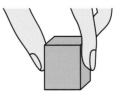

Piece of kitchen sponge

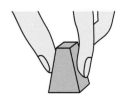

Make-up wedge

7. Dip the sponge into the paint. Blot on the paper towel to remove excess paint and work the paint into the sponge until the paint on the towel looks dull. Stenciling is a dry-brush technique. Too much paint means a sloppy stencil.

8. Hold the fabric down with your free hand to stabilize it. Still holding the sponge on the sides with your other hand, begin applying the paint around the edge of the stencil opening. Use either an up-and-down motion, called stippling, or a round-and-round motion, called rouging. Add more paint as needed, always remembering to blot on the paper towel before applying to the fabric. Gradually work toward the center of the opening with the same motion until the fabric is covered. Keep the paint at the center of the design a little lighter than that at the outside edges. You don't want to conceal the fabric surface totally; just cover with color and create a crisp edge.

9. To add another color to the design, use another sponge. Continue stenciling in the same manner until all the open areas are filled in with paint.

10. When the design is complete, carefully peel off the stencil.

11. Wait until the first layer is dry (usually in a few minutes), then place stencil #2 on the painted design so that the traced lines match up with the outlines of the areas you already painted. Place a paper towel over the new stencil and press to fuse. Stencil in the same manner. Use a fresh sponge, start with the edges, and work toward the center. Repeat this step for any additional layers.

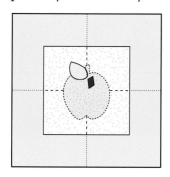

Line up traced lines with painted areas, cover with paper towel, and fuse.

12. Cover your ironing board with a press cloth of white tissue paper or muslin. Place the painted surface of the fabric face down on the press cloth. To heat-set the acrylic paint, iron the back of the fabric with a dry iron set to "cotton" for 1 minute. Ironing on the back first sets the paint the best. Turn the stenciled piece over, cover the painted surface with paper or fabric, and iron the front for another minute or two.

NOTE: Fabric dyes can also be heat-set by drying in the dryer on "high" or "cotton" for 20 minutes.

Little House Project

Supplies

- Scrap of fabric, at least 6" x 6", for background
- 2-part House stencil (page 11)
- Acrylic paint in 3 colors

Remember: Less paint is better!

Directions

1. Cut a 6" x 6" piece of background fabric.
2. Follow steps 2–8 on pages 14–15, using your house/chimney color in steps 5–8.
3. Carefully remove stencil #1 and allow paint to dry.
4. Complete step 11, using stencil #2 (door/windows/roof). Use light or white paint for the windows and dark paint for the door and roof.
5. Remove stencil #2 and admire your stenciled house.
6. Press to heat-set (step 12).

Now your house just needs the details described in the next chapter. Let's get going!

Can You Draw a Crooked Line? Then You Can Scribble the Details!

Get ready for the most dramatic and exciting technique in this book: pen work.
It's easy to do and will literally transform your stencil before your eyes! Let's talk about supplies first.

My Favorite Pens

Black Markers

Sharpie Fine Point and Ultra Fine Point permanent pens are the best for outlines and details. These Sanford-brand pens can be bought at most office-supply stores, discount stores, and drugstores. They say "not for letter writing or cloth" on the label, but I use them on fabric all the time. I use the Fine Point for outlining and the Ultra Fine Point for faces and other small details. Since this pen is not designed for use on fabric, test for bleeding first and draw on the painted design, rather than the fabric background, as much as possible.

Colored Markers

The colored markers used for the popular memory books are the same kind I use on fabric and stencils. Make sure they are "permanent" or "pigment" ink, not "washable" or "watercolor" markers. Marvy, Zig, and Y&C FabricMate are all excellent and long-lasting. Buy gray and brown to start, then add other colors as you become a stenciling addict!

Paint Pens

You can use metallic paint pens from the craft, stamp, or office-supply store; just be sure to write only on the painted surface.

Little House Project

Supplies

- Stenciled house
- Wide- and narrow-tipped black permanent pens
- Colored markers or pencils in gray and brown
- Paper
- Fabric scrap

See how outlines, scribbles, and shading transform even the most basic stencil.

Test pens before using them on fabric. Sharpies are my favorite black permanent markers.

Directions

1. Place a piece of paper under the stenciled house in case the pen bleeds through.
2. Test the pen on the scrap of fabric to check for bleeding.
3. Using the Fine Point Sharpie pen, draw a dashed or solid line around the outer edge of the house. Connect the roof line at the intersection of the chimney and roof.

Outline the stenciled house
in black pen.

4. Use the pen to fill in spaces where the painted areas do not quite connect, for example, draw the line between the roof edge and the top of the house.
5. Next, outline the internal design lines. Correct uneven edges by drawing over or right next to them with the pen. Add shingles to the roof, bricks to the chimney, panels and doorknob to the door, and panes to the windows. Add other details as desired.

6. Switch to a narrow-tipped black pen, such as an Ultra Fine Point or a #1 or #3 permanent marking pen. Bleeding is not a concern here since the pen stays on the paint. Add thin squiggles all over the house as shown.

7. Using any colored pen or pencil you have on hand (see facing page), shade in the areas indicated in the illustration below. I used a brown pen for the house, bricks, roof, and door, and a gray pen for the windows. To shade, draw just inside the pen outline.

Next, we will make your darling stenciled house into a quilt!

Can You Stitch a Seam?
Then You Can Make a Quilt!

Growing up, I used to frustrate my mother with my "short-term" sewing techniques (tape, staples, safety pins). Now I know how to sew correctly, but I still like to use fast and easy tricks to get the job done. And there are so many of them in quiltmaking today! Let me show you how to make a cute little quilt out of your stenciled house.

Let us run through the essentials before we get to the project itself.

Supplies

• Several fat quarters of fabric to audition for borders, backing, and binding (see page 12 for information about choosing fabrics)

• A piece of batting cut a little larger than the finished quilt measurement

• Sewing machine (optional)

• Transparent nylon thread for machine quilting (optional)

• White quilting thread for hand quilting (optional)—Gutermann all-cotton and cotton-wrapped polyester are excellent.

• Sewing-machine needles (Schmetz, universal #12 for piecing and #10 to #14 for machine quilting), and/or Between or Quilting needle (#9 works best for me)

Trimming

When you stenciled the house, you tried to center it on the fabric. Sometimes stencils are a little off-center, so first trim the fabric to center the painted design. Don't worry; there is extra fabric built in for this.

1. Using a rotary cutter, ruler, and mat, trim the bottom edge of your fabric ½" from the bottom of your stenciled house.

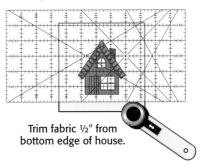

Trim fabric ½" from bottom edge of house.

2. Rotate the ruler 90° so one edge lies along the right side of your fabric. Align a set of horizontal markings along the bottom edge of the fabric, then slide the ruler from side to side until the roof tip hits the ½" mark on the right side. Trim.

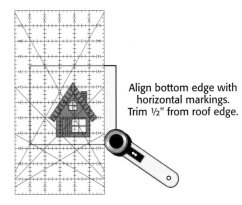

Align bottom edge with horizontal markings. Trim ½" from roof edge.

3. Rotate the ruler 90° and repeat, trimming ½" from the roof peak and using the right edge as your guide.

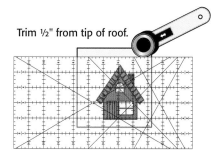

Trim ½" from tip of roof.

4. Rotate the ruler 90° and repeat, trimming ½" from the roof tip on the left side of the house. This time, make sure the horizontal markings line up with both the top and bottom edges.

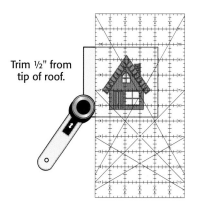

Trim ½" from tip of roof.

Your stenciled house should be perfectly centered and your corners square.

Adding Borders

1. Make sure your machine is working well and set the stitch length to 12 to 15 stitches to the inch.

   NOTE: The sewing machine is fast, but if you like to hand sew, go ahead and stitch away.

2. Pick a border fabric by laying the stenciled piece on each fat quarter in turn.

3. Decide how wide you want the borders to be. I usually make mine 1" to 3" wide. To do this, lay the stencil on the border fabric and fold back the border fabric until you get a width you like. Measure, then add ½" for trimming and seam allowances. This is your border-strip width.

4. From your fat quarter, cut 2 border strips the width you determined in step 3.

   NOTE: If you plan to use one fat quarter for the borders, binding, and backing, conserve fabric by cutting the border strips along the short edge of the fabric.

5. Measure your trimmed stencil from top to bottom through the center of the design. Cut 2 border strips this length.

6. Pin the borders to the sides of the quilt center, lining up the top and bottom edges. If you have to stretch the borders a little, that is fine. I only pin at the top and the bottom.

7. Stitch the borders to the quilt center, using a ¼" seam allowance.

Side borders

8. Press the seams on the wrong side to set the stitching. Open out and press the seam allowances toward the borders.

9. Measure across the center of your quilt from side to side, including the borders. Cut 2 border strips this length.

10. Pin the borders to the top and bottom of the quilt, lining up the side edges.

11. Stitch the borders to the quilt, using a ¼" seam allowance. Press as described in step 8.

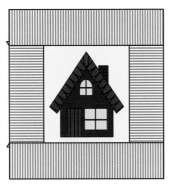

Top and bottom borders

Your little piece of stenciled fabric is now a quilt top!

Preparing the Quilt Sandwich

1. Lay the little quilt top, right side up, on the batting and backing; trim the backing and batting, leaving 1" all around (leave 2" for larger quilts).

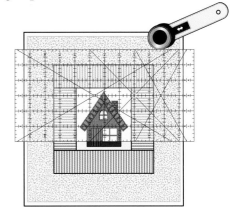

2. Press the quilt sandwich from the back, using a medium iron with steam. This makes the layers lie flat and helps them stick together during quilting and binding.

Quilting

Quilting makes the stenciled design pouf out and look more like appliqué. Remember, part of the quilt will be covered by embellishments, so don't waste time on too much quilting. I stitch around the figure and perhaps around some of the small details. Because I want to finish these little quilts as quickly as possible, I usually combine hand and machine quilting. When I hand quilt pieces this small, I just hold the quilt instead of using a hoop.

1. Pin the quilt sandwich together in the center and around the outside edge with long straight pins. To baste a larger project, see the box opposite.

2. Thread your sewing machine. I use transparent nylon in the top and all-purpose thread in the bobbin. Set the stitch length where you like it for machine quilting and

loosen the tension a little. Stitch in-the-ditch around the inside of the border. Begin in a corner with a backstitch and end in the same corner, again backstitching to lock your stitches. If you're new to machine quilting, stitching in-the-ditch means placing your quilting right in the seam. Pull the thread ends to the back, knot, and clip them close to the fabric.

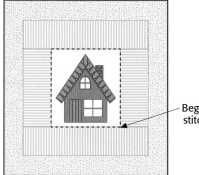

Begin and end stitching here.

Basting

The Little House sample project is small and easy to manipulate, but for larger projects you'll want to baste the layers before you quilt to prevent them from shifting. Baste in a grid, beginning in the middle and working out toward the edge. Space basting lines 4" to 5" apart. Use thread for hand-quilted projects and safety pins or a basting gun for machine quilting.

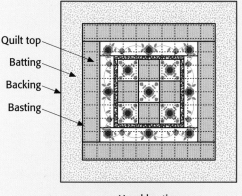

Quilt top
Batting
Backing
Basting

Hand basting

For hand quilting, I like to fold the backing to the front of the quilt and baste it down over the exposed batting to protect the raw edges.

3. Hand stitch around the stenciled design. If you feel comfortable machine quilting around a small design, do it! Or, if you don't want to machine quilt at all, don't. Use your talents as you see fit.

Binding the Quilt

In 1987 I took a miniature quilting class from Becky Schaffer. She taught a binding method that gives you wonderful, perfect corners with no fuss or muss. I use this method on all my quilts, whether tiny or king size. The following instructions may seem long—it's easier than it looks.

1. When you are finished quilting, press the quilt on both sides. Using a rotary cutter and ruler, trim the batting and backing even with the quilt top. Use your ruler to check that the corners are square. Trim as necessary.

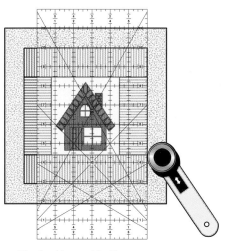

Trim backing and batting even with the edges of the quilt top.

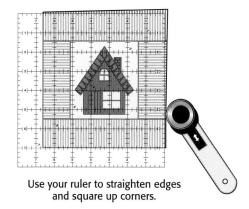

Use your ruler to straighten edges and square up corners.

2. Choose a binding fabric. Cut binding strips 1¾" wide (2" for larger quilts).

3. Measure through the center of your quilt from top to bottom. Cut 2 binding strips this length.

4. With right sides together and the binding strips on top, pin the binding to the sides of the quilt top. Make sure the short ends of the binding are even with the edges of the quilt. If necessary, stretch the strips a bit.

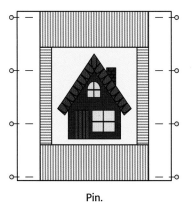

Pin.

5. Stitch, using a ¼" seam allowance. (For larger quilts with 2"-wide bindings, use an exact ⅜"-wide seam allowance.) Press the seam allowances toward the binding.

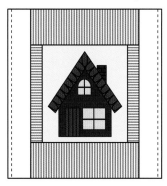

Stitch.

6. Turn the quilt over and fold the long raw edges of the bindings in to meet the raw edges of the quilt.

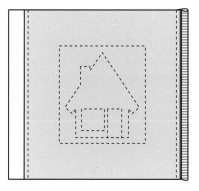

7. Fold the bindings in again, this time bringing the folded edges you created in the last step over the seam allowances so it covers the stitching on the quilt back. Press. Pin at both ends as shown while holding the folded edges flat against the quilt back.

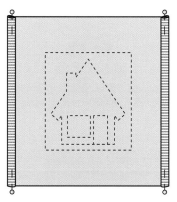

8. Measure across the center of the quilt from side to side, including the binding. Add 3½" to this measurement and cut 2 binding strips this length.

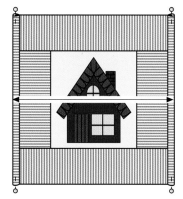

9. Fold the quilt in half lengthwise to determine the centers of the top and bottom edges. Pin to mark. Fold the 2 binding strips from step 8 in half crosswise to determine their centers. Crease to mark.

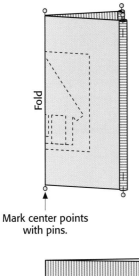

Mark center points
with pins.

Fold top and bottom bindings
in half and crease.

10. Pin the binding to the quilt top with right sides together and the center creases at the center pins.

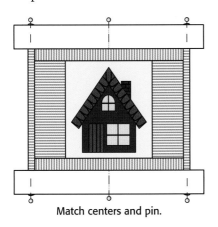

Match centers and pin.

11. Fold the ends of the top and bottom bindings to the back of the quilt, over the pinned side bindings. Pin through the top and bottom bindings, making sure they're wrapped tightly around the edges of the quilt.

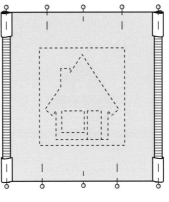

Fold over snugly and pin.

12. Sew from one folded-over edge to the other, backstitching at the ends and sewing through all layers. Use a ¼" seam allowance for mini quilts, or a ⅜" seam allowance for larger quilts. Remove pins.

13. Fold the top and bottom binding strips away from the quilt, turning the wrapped ends right side out. Press.

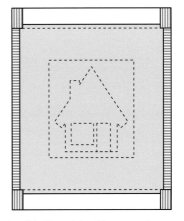

Turn bindings right side out and press.

14. Fold, press, and pin the top and bottom binding as described in steps 6 and 7 on page 22.

15. Hand stitch the binding down, making sure it covers the stitching line on the back.

Hand stitch binding on wrong side.

Little House Project

Supplies

- Stenciled house
- Fat quarter of fabric for borders and binding
- 10" x 10" piece of batting

Follow the directions on trimming, adding borders, quilting, and binding on pages 18–24. Admire your quick Little House quilt.

I hope I have convinced you to continue with stenciling. It is fast, fun, and easy. Next, embellishments add personality to your little quilt.

Can You Sew on a Button?
Then You Can Add Embellishments!

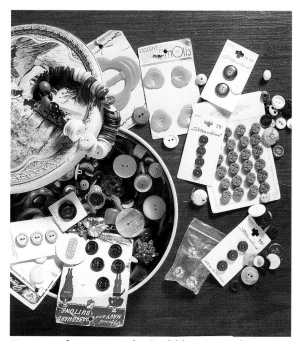

Treasures from my mother's old button tin: buttons, beads, and charms

Buttons

Button collecting is a major obsession of mine. I buy other people's button boxes and love to go through the treasures my students bring to class. If you have special buttons, you are going to love embellishments. If you don't have special buttons, we'll get you into the habit of collecting them.

Check both sides of buttons. The backs can be even better than the fronts and are especially great for writing since they're smoother. I sew buttons on with quilting thread or cotton crochet thread: the fewer the stitches, the better.

The following are some fun and unusual ways to use buttons.

• Combine a big button and some beads to make a dangling string of beads as follows:
1. Thread your needle with quilting thread and knot one end.
2. Bring the needle up through your project and through the button.
3. String several beads (bells, buttons, charms) onto the needle. Loop the thread around the outside of the last bead, then run the needle back through the other beads, the button, and the fabric. Knot the thread on the back of the project.

String beads on thread.

Loop thread around top bead, then back through.

• Knot a scrap of fabric and sew on top of a button.

• Layer buttons on top of each other. For example, I took the Big Blah Button (BBB) in the photo and sewed a contrasting smaller button on top.

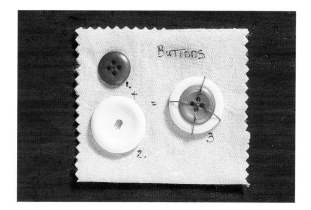

Buttons embellished with fabric, beads, bells, and ribbon

Button flowers

Ladybug

• Make button flowers with ribbon leaves. Make 2 ribbon loops and tie in the center with thread. Sew a button on top of the loops, then add a bead for the flower center.

• For another type of button flower, embroider stems and green leaves with a lazy daisy stitch and top with buttons and beads.

Drawing and Writing on Buttons

Did you know you could paint and write on buttons? I do it all the time. Use Sharpies, which don't smear. When dry, set the ink by spraying with Krylon Matte Finish. To experiment with button drawing, try your hand at the ladybug, peppermint candy, and other designs that follow.

Ladybug

1. Choose a small red button with 2 holes.
2. With a black Sharpie, draw a straight line across the button, ⅓ of the way down the button at about the first hole.

3. For the bug's head, color in the top ⅓ with a black Sharpie.
4. Draw a line down the center of the button from the head area to make the wings. Draw random dots on the wings.

5. Let the ink dry for 24 hours, then spray lightly with Krylon.
6. Sew the button onto a quilt, then draw antennae on the fabric background, using the Sharpie or marker.

Peppermint Candy

Use a Sharpie Ultra Fine Point pen to divide button into sections. Color every other section with a red marker.

Snowflakes

Use a gold paint pen to draw 2 Xs on a button, then add small intersecting lines and pointed ends for a crystalline effect.

Message Buttons

This is a great way to say, "Happy Birthday" or "Merry Christmas." What about writing a quilt's title on a button and sewing it to the front?

1. Pick a flat, smooth button. Button backs are sometimes flatter than the fronts.
2. Trace around the button on a piece of paper to practice writing the message and to plan word placement.
3. Write the message on the button with a Sharpie Ultra Fine point pen, let dry for 24 hours, and spray with Krylon.

Button Faces

Skin-tone buttons in pink, tan, or brown are perfect for children's faces. Wood buttons are good, too. Make sure the button has only two holes, unless you want to depict four-eyed alien children.

1. Draw in hair and eyelashes with the Ultra Fine Point black Sharpie. Just make scribbles and lines.

2. Color in hair with a colored marker.
3. Add a little dashed circle for the cheeks. Color in with a pink marker.

Peppermint candy

Snowflakes

Message buttons

Button faces

4. Connect the cheeks with a little black U or V as shown.

Isn't she cute? If you want to make a boy, put a hat on him.

Draw line above eyes; add bill.　　Finish like other face.

5. Let your buttons dry for 24 hours, then spray with Krylon.

   NOTE: If you mess up a button, just turn it over and sew it onto something else. Our secret!

Bows

Of all the embellishments I use, people most often comment on these meandering ribbon bows. I learned this technique from Ellen Mosbarger, who taught Victorian appliqué at my local quilt shop. She used French knots to anchor the ribbon. French knots got boring, so I made it easier!

Ribbon embellishments

Tacked Ribbon Bow

This technique works best on narrow ribbons 1⁄16" to 1⁄4" wide. Use inexpensive ribbon; you want the plain satin type, not picot-edged or grosgrain.

1. Cut a 14" piece of 1⁄4"-wide ribbon. Tie it in a big, loopy bow. Make the loops twice as big as you want them to end up.

2. Thread a #9 Sharp or Embroidery needle with quilting thread. Knot the end. Place the bow on the stenciled design and tack through the center knot with a couple of stitches. End with the thread on the back of the quilt.

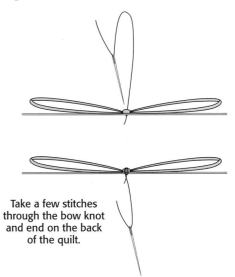

Take a few stitches through the bow knot and end on the back of the quilt.

3. Bring the needle up through the quilt under a ribbon loop for your first stitch. I start at the top left of the bow about 1" from the knot. With your thumb on top of the ribbon loop, push the ribbon toward the knot

slightly until it bulges up from the surface. Tack the ribbon next to your thumb. Pull the thread tight, causing the ribbon to gather up a little bit. Don't pull so tight that the fabric bunches up.

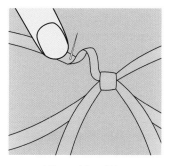

While pushing ribbon,
bring needle up from back.

4. Move your thumb back about 1" (¼" to ½" on smaller bows), push the ribbon up, tack it down, and pull tight. As you continue tacking and gathering around the loop, the ribbon begins to meander. This is the look you want.

5. Gather and tack both loops in this manner, then do the same with the tendrils, which can meander across the surface as desired.

6. Finish off the tendrils by wrapping the thread around the ribbon twice ¼" from the end of the ribbon. Secure to the quilt and knot on the back. Trim the ribbon ends at a nice angle.

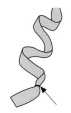

Wrap the thread around
the tendril end to cinch.

Trim end.

Couched Ribbon Bow

To make couched ribbon bows, wrap the thread around the ribbon like a lasso and secure to the fabric, instead of stitching through the ribbon. This dramatic and easy technique works especially well with wider ribbons and fabric strips, but can be used on all sizes.

Couching Stitch

Bring needle up through fabric, wind around ribbon, bring down through fabric, and pull tight. Place couching stitches at regular intervals around loops and down tendrils. Finish ends as for tacked bows.

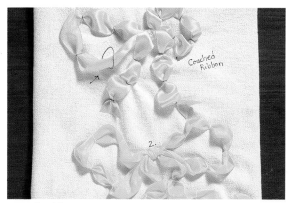

Couched bows

Torn-Fabric Bow

Try tearing narrow strips of fabric and using them instead of ribbon to make meandering bows. The technique is the same, but the bow loops need to be three times larger than the desired finished size.

Torn-fabric bow

Concertina Roses

Marlene Peterman taught me to make these beautiful ribbon roses. The technique, called "concertina rose," appears in many Crazy quilt and embellishment books. I remember making these roses out of stiff gift-wrapping ribbon to decorate presents in the '50s. The technique is still the same.

> **NOTE:** Use plain ½" satin ribbon to start— not picot-edged or grosgrain.

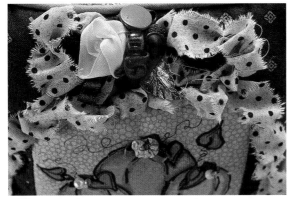
Little concertina roses

Directions

1. Cut a 12" piece of ribbon. (Wider ribbons require more length, narrower ribbons less.)

2. Thread a needle with quilting thread, knot, and set aside. If you don't do this now, you will have to hold the finished rose in your teeth as you fumble with the needle and thread.

3. In the center of the ribbon, fold the left end down to form a miter.

4. Take the right end of the ribbon and fold it straight across the miter fold. Hold the fold down with your thumb.

5. Fold ribbon on the bottom over to the top.

6. Continue folding the ribbon, alternating sides until you have made at least 10 folds.

NOTE: The wider the ribbon, the more folds you will need to make for a nice, full rose.

7. You should now have a stack of folds with two ribbon tails. With the thumb and index finger of one hand, hold the tails close to the stack. Pin the tails together. Hold the stack in the other hand.

8. Holding onto the tails at the pin, let go of the stack. The ribbon should expand like an accordion (thus the name concertina rose).

9. Take out the pin. With your right hand, take one of the ribbon tails (either one is OK) and slowly pull while still holding the other tail at the base of the folds. Look at the top of the folds as you pull and you will see a rose begin to form.

10. When the center of the rose compacts into itself, *stop!* More pulling will cause the folds to disappear, losing the rose.

11. With the threaded and knotted needle, go down into the center of the rose from the top, catching the tails in the stitch.

12. Push the needle back up through the rose and out the top. Push the needle down through the rose again and wrap the thread around both tails a couple of times. Knot the thread and cut it.

13. Trim the ribbon tails at the base of the rose, leaving ½" to hold on to.

To attach the rose to a project, I sew through the center of the rose and through the fabric a couple of times, knotting the thread on the back. You can also glue roses to your design with fabric glue.

Rosettes

I like to use up every little scrap of ribbon, so I devised a way to use the cut-off tails of folded roses. This makes a nice rosette and is even easier than the folded rose.

Directions

1. Thread a needle with quilting thread, knotting the end.
2. Cut a 3" to 4" length of ribbon (6" for a wider ribbon). Sew a running stitch along one long edge of the ribbon. Don't worry about making perfect, even stitches. Stitch to the end of the ribbon and leave the needle in the thread.

3. Hold both ends of the ribbon in one hand and pull the thread slowly to gather.
4. Pull the gathers tight, then stitch through both ends of the ribbon to hold them together. Tie the thread off under the rosette.

5. To sew the rosette to your design, sew a bead or button larger than the hole to the rosette center. Tack the edges, if necessary, to make the rosette lie flat. You can also glue the flower and button to the fabric.

Ribbon Leaves

Use a 4" length of ¼"- or ⅛"-wide ribbon to make simple leaves like the ones used with button and bead flowers.

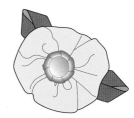

1. Bring the ends together to form a twisted loop.

2. Stitch through both ends at the bottom of the loop and pull to gather.

3. Wrap the thread tightly around the ends, over the gathering stitches, and knot. Trim ends ¼" from the knot.
4. To sew the leaf to your design, tuck the ends under a rose and tack down at the knot. The loop becomes a little green leaf peeking out from under the flower.

No-Sew Yo-Yos

Now for the amazing folded yo-yo. These are not my invention; I found them in *The Gathering*, a wonderful book of folk-art quilts and goodies by Kindred Spirits. I love their off-center flower look. They are super simple to make—no sewing!

1. Cut a circle of fabric approximately twice the size of the finished yo-yo.
2. Fold the circle in half, then in half again. Crease the folds, then unfold.

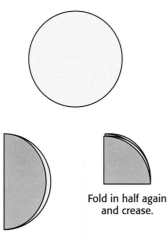

Fold circle in half
and crease.

Fold in half again
and crease.

Unfold circle.

3. Place the circle on your work surface with the wrong side up and the creases running straight up and down and side to side. Fold the top of the circle down to the center. Press the fold you just created.

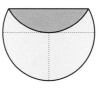

4. Now fold the point formed by the previous fold in to meet the center. Press.

5. Continue around the circle, bringing the corners in to the center and creasing until you have completed the circle. You may have to fudge a little to get the final point sharp. You should end up with a slightly asymmetrical yo-yo.

6. Sew a button in the center to make a flower. Use it to embellish a flower design or the center of a button cluster.

Little House Project

Supplies

- 20" piece of ¼"-wide ribbon, in a color that contrasts with the border fabric and coordinates with the paint colors
- Several small to large buttons in colors that go with your quilt
- Sharpie Ultra Fine Point pen
- Krylon Matte Finish for sealing ink on buttons
- Small seed bead or snap for doorknob
- Charms, beads, and anything else you may like to put on your quilt
- Quilting thread in color to match ribbon

Directions

1. To make the ribbon bow in the middle of the top border, follow the directions on pages 28–29. Place the loops in the border, and the tendrils falling on either side of the center square.
2. Choose a large button for the center of your bow.
3. Audition other buttons to go around the center by setting them on the bow. Are they too bold, too shiny, or too dull? Choose 2 or 3 buttons in different sizes for each side. Do any beads and charms you have go with the buttons? Use them, too!
4. Sew the large center button over the bow knot, using your needle and quilting thread. Go through each hole a couple of times and knot the thread when you're done. Instead of cutting the thread, run it through the quilt and come up for the next button. Don't worry about stitches showing on the back.
5. Sew on the next button, overlapping the large button on one side, either under or over the large button. Go to the opposite side and sew another button overlapping the large button. Continue going back and forth, adding buttons, beads, etc. When you like the arrangement, knot the thread to finish.
6. With your Sharpie Ultra Fine Point pen, write something on a button, such as Home Sweet Home, Home Is Where Your Heart Is, or your family name. Let the button dry for 24 hours and then spray with Krylon. Sew a button to a corner of the border.
7. Sew on a little bead or snap for a doorknob.
8. Sign and date the back.

You have just completed your first stenciled and embellished mini quilt. Wasn't it fun? Want to do another? Go to the project section and jump in!

Not Mistakes—Opportunities!

Boo-boos, mistakes. Oh, no! We all make them, and we have to learn to deal with them. On one quilt I was making, I ran out of the terrific black border fabric with colored stars. It was late, all the stores were closed, and of course I had a deadline. What did I do? I used a similar black-and-white star print, but used my fabric pens to color the white stars to match the original border fabric! Students always get a laugh when I point it out to them, but no one ever notices it otherwise. This is what I call a creative opportunity.

We tend to be hypercritical of our own mistakes, pointing them out to others who would never have noticed them. As a teacher, I point out my own mistakes so students can learn to accept the inconsistencies of stenciling and quilting, but you don't need to! Keep mum and no one will ever know what is under that button or section of pen work.

Sometimes a project really isn't worth saving and should be done over, but first try a few of these remedies for common problems.

• Too much paint gives stencils uneven edges and a globby look. Outlining, details, and shading usually even up the edges and direct the eye away from the area (page 17). Notice how the bright white dots on the star in the photo distract you from the uneven paint inside the design.

• It's difficult to line up multilayered stencils exactly. A good outline almost always fills in the open space (page 17).

Misaligned stencils leave open spaces between pumpkins. Outlining and shading cover them up.

Outlining and details draw the eye away from uneven paint and sloppy edges.

• Another trick is to fill in the space with a fabric pen in a color that either matches the paint or is slightly darker. *Important:* Don't just shade the open area; shade adjacent areas as well to integrate the shading into the design.

• You can even shift the stencil and dab the open space with a little bit of paint, then outline and even up the area. Wait until the stencil is completed and dry. Now move the stencil to expose the unpainted area. If the area is large, iron the stencil down; if not, just hold it tight against the fabric as you gently apply more paint.

Shifting the roof stencil to one side and repainting covers the open area.

• Sometimes paint strays over the *outer* edge of the stencil. I call these marks "shadows." They can be turned into clouds or ground by swiping the area with a dry sponge in the appropriate color.

Green paint swept on with a dry brush covers the yellow shadow below the beehive and creates grass.

TIP: If you catch mistakes while the paint is fresh, you may be able to remove some or all of it by scrubbing with a piece of muslin or a white eraser.

• Messy-looking stencils can be rehabilitated with embellishments and pen work. In the top photo at right, see how the layers overlap on the snowman design and how splotchy the white paint looks? A few embellishments make the finished project look great, as shown in the bottom photo.

• Is something the wrong color? Paint over it. Position the stencil on top of the area and re-stencil in white or a lighter color. Wait for the paint to dry and paint with the new color. This may leave a small outline of the undercoat showing, but line work and shading can cover it. Sometimes a white outline actually looks like an intended highlight.

If you can't find a trick that helps, begin again. It's only a small bit of fabric, and stenciling is fast. I throw things away or put them aside to use in another project all the time.

This snowman's head shows through his hat, and his nose is uneven.

Here's our untidy snowman reborn. Black pen lines and gold paint cover the exposed white paint on the hat, black pen markings on the face give the snowman a cute expression and define the uneven nose, and an overall black outline and gray shading add dimension.

Stencil Projects

You have finished your little house and are ready to continue stenciling. Little quilts and ornaments are quick, easy, and fun. Pillows take a bit more time and fabric but are worth the effort.

Begin by reviewing the stenciling directions on pages 8–17. In addition to the materials listed for each project, you will need the items listed in the Master Supply List below.

Master Supply List

- Freezer paper
- Pencil
- Scissors or craft knife
- Rotary cutter, acrylic ruler, and cutting mat (optional but highly recommended)
- Ruler (if not using rotary equipment)
- Sponges
- Paper towels
- Paper plates
- Iron, ironing board, and press cloth
- Sharpie Fine Point and Ultra Fine Point black permanent pens
- Paper
- Sewing machine (optional)
- Cotton or cotton-wrapped polyester thread
- Transparent nylon thread for machine quilting
- White quilting thread
- Between or quilting needle (#9 works best for me) for hand quilting
- Pins

NOTE: Does one of the projects not quite fit your mood? Substitute any of the stencils at the back of the book!

Winter Snowman Pillow

Finished size: 7" x 7½"

Snowmen are fun to have around all winter, so make this one in colors other than red and green.
I chose bright blue with multicolored stars for fun. The borders are a little different from the ones
on the House quilt, but just as simple.

Materials

- 4½" x 6" piece of blue fabric for background
- 2 strips of black-and-white checked fabric, each 2" x 7", for border
- 2 strips of bright flower fabric, each 2" x 10", for border
- 10" x 10" piece of fabric for backing
- ½" x 8" strip of torn fabric
- 2 pieces of batting, each 10" x 10" (see Tip below)
- Small amount of fiberfill
- Acrylic craft paint in white, brown, yellow, and orange
- Gray, brown, and pink permanent fabric markers
- 2 small black snaps
- 1 large white button
- Krylon Matte Finish
- Craft glue (optional)
- 1 small red button
- 1 silver heart pony bead
- 1 pink star pony bead
- Several colored beads
- 1 small brass star charm
- 1 medium pom-pom
- 2 small pom-poms
- ½ yd. of ⅜"-wide black-and-white checked ribbon
- 1 piece of ¼"-wide yellow ribbon, 6" long
- 1 medium black bead

TIP: This tip is from my sister-in-law Brenda Garnas. Sew batting to the pillow back, as well as the front—when you stuff the pillow, it will be smooth and soft.

Stenciling

1. Using the pattern on page 43, make a 2-part snowman stencil.
2. Center stencil #1 on the blue fabric, fuse, and stencil in white. It may take more than one coat of paint to cover the background well. Use several light coats instead of trying to coat it heavily the first time. Remove stencil #1.
3. Align stencil #2 with the edges of the snowman's body. Fuse. Apply a thin layer of white paint in all openings, paint the arms brown, adding a little white paint for snow. Stencil the hat yellow and his nose orange.
4. Press to heat-set (page 15).
5. Referring to the drawing below and the photograph on page 39, add pen-work details. Draw the face as described on pages 27–28. For shading, use a gray marker on the white areas and a brown one on the yellow. Color the cheeks with the pink marker.

Pen-work details

Construction

1. Trim the background ½" from the snowman on all sides (pages 18–19).
2. Measure the background across the center from side to side. Cut 1 of your 2" x 7" strips of checked fabric this length. Sew to the bottom of the background. Press toward the border.

3. Measure the background through the center from top to bottom, including the bottom border. Cut your other strip of checked fabric this length. Sew to the right side of the background. Press toward the border.

4. Following the same procedure, add the flower fabric border strips to the top and left side of the background. Press. Your snowman is now a pillow top.

Measure, cut, and add borders.

5. Layer the pillow top with 1 piece of batting. Press with a warm iron.
6. Machine quilt in-the-ditch around the border seams (page 21). Hand or machine quilt around the snowman.
7. Stack your backing fabric, right side down; remaining piece of batting; and quilted pillow top, right side up. Trim the edges even with the pillow top, then re-stack as shown.

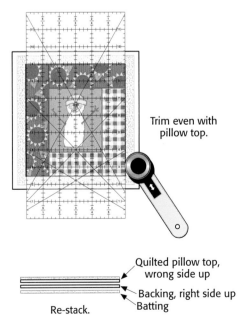

Trim even with pillow top.

Quilted pillow top, wrong side up

Backing, right side up

Batting

Re-stack.

8. Sew around the pillow with a ½" seam, leaving a 3" opening for turning and stuffing.

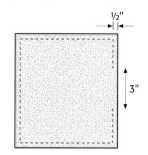

9. Trim the corners and turn the pillow cover right side out.

Embellishment

Embellish your pillow while you can still put your hand inside to sew.

1. Sew snaps on the face for eyes.
2. From your strip of torn fabric, cut a 1½" length and stitch to the snowman's neck as a muffler. Cut a 5" piece, tie a large double knot in the center, and tack it to the muffler as a tie. Cut a small piece of torn fabric, tie a knot in the middle, and sew to the side of his hat. Don't worry about turning under the edges on these; you want them ragged.

3. Write "LET IT SNOW" on the large white button with a Sharpie Ultra Fine Point pen (page 27). Let dry for 24 hours, then spray with Krylon to set. Layer the white button with a small red button and sew them on the pillow at lower right with a string of beads (page 25), ending with a star bead.
4. Referring to the photograph on page 39, sew beads and star charm to the left arm. Sew or glue medium pom-pom in right hand for snowball and 2 small pom-poms at sides of head for earmuffs.
5. Make a tacked ribbon bow from checked ribbon(page 28) and sew to top left corner.
6. Make a rosette (page 31) from yellow ribbon and sew to the ribbon bow with a black button in the center.
7. Sign and date the back.

Finishing

Stuff the pillow with fiberfill and whipstitch the opening closed. Your little snowman is sure to bring you joy during those cold winter months.

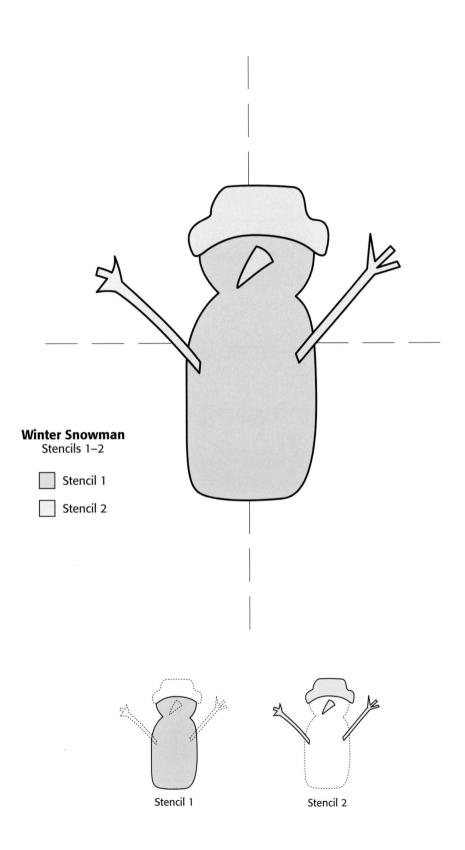

Winter Snowman
Stencils 1–2

◼ Stencil 1

◻ Stencil 2

Stencil 1

Stencil 2

43

Bees and Hive Little Quilt

Finished size: 6½" x 6"

Bees and hives are the essence of summer. What fun to make a little quilt full of busy, buzzy bees and heart flowers! This little quilt is made just like the Little House quilt on page 7, with a few extra bees stenciled in the borders and a contrasting binding.

Materials

- 5" x 5" piece of printed muslin for background
- 1 fat quarter of peach print for borders and backing
- Mini-stripe fabric for binding
- 8" x 8" piece of batting
- Acrylic craft paint in black, gold, white, brown, pink, and green
- Light brown, gray, and yellow permanent fabric markers
- ½ yd. of ⅛"-wide peach ribbon
- ½ yd. of ¾"-wide ivory ribbon
- 1 belt buckle or fancy button
- Quilting thread in colors to match ribbons
- Small bee charm

Stenciling

1. Using the pattern on page 47, make a 2-part beehive stencil and a 2-part extra bee stencil.
2. Center stencil #1 (beehive) on the muslin square, fuse, and stencil in gold.
3. Align stencil #2 with the edges of the beehive. Fuse. Stencil the bee bodies in gold, bee wings in white, entrance in brown, heart flowers in pink, and leaves in green. Add tiny white dots to the flowers with a pin dipped in white paint. (Extra bees are added after borders are attached.)

4. Press to heat-set (page 15).
5. Referring to the drawing below and the photograph on the facing page, add pen-work details. Use a black Sharpie pen on the bees (stripes, scribbles, and antennae), entrance, flower stamens, and leaf centers. Shade hive with a light brown marker, and white bee wings with a gray marker.

Pen-work details

Construction

1. Trim the background around the design (pages 18–19).
2. Cut 1¾"-wide border strips from the peach print fabric. Measure, cut, stitch, and press as described in steps 5–11 on pages 19–20.
3. Layer the quilt top with batting and backing and press (page 20).
4. Machine quilt in-the-ditch (page 21) around border seams. Hand or machine quilt around hive.
5. Press, trim, and square up the quilt (page 21).
6. Using the mini-stripe fabric, cut and add binding as described in steps 2–15 on pages 22–24. Cut strips so that the stripes run across them the short way.

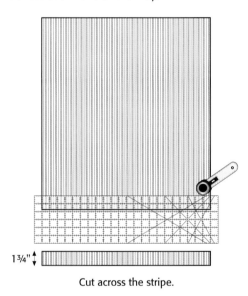

1¾"

Cut across the stripe.

7. Stencil extra bees onto the border, using the extra bee stencil on the facing page. Outline and add details as before. Draw tiny free-form bees as shown.

Draw free-form bees
this size.

(Drawings below are enlarged
to show detail.)

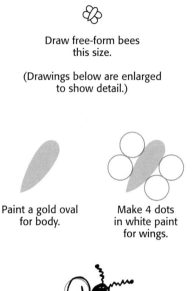

Paint a gold oval
for body.

Make 4 dots
in white paint
for wings.

In black, draw a circle for the head,
scribble stripes on back,
draw lines on wings, and
squiggle antennae with dots at the ends.

Embellishment

1. Using the peach ribbon and matching thread, sew a large, tacked ribbon bow to top of hive (page 28). Sew a small bee charm to knot.
2. Thread the buckle onto the ivory ribbon and center it. Stitch the buckle to the quilt at lower left, then meander ribbon out to each side and couch with matching thread as you would the tendrils on a bow (page 29).
3. If you want to add further embellishments, attach a bee button or a bee painted on a plain button.
4. Sign and date your work.

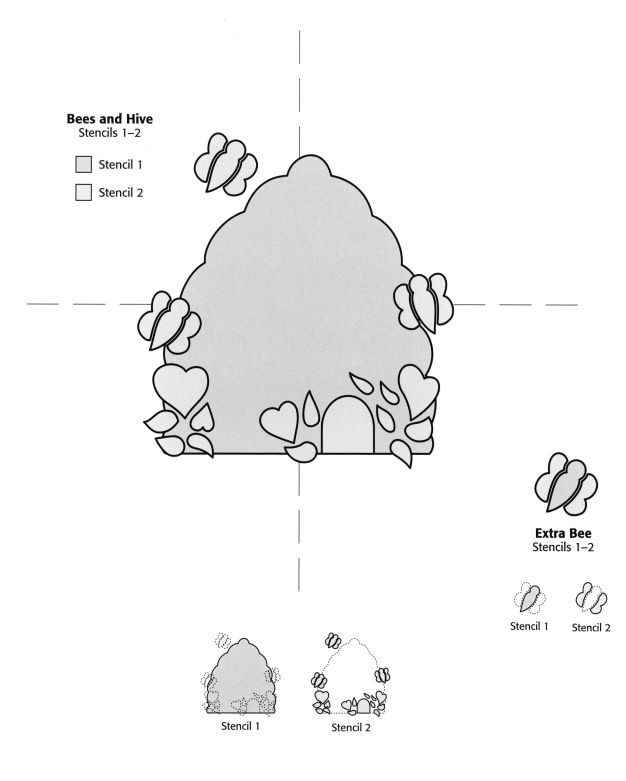

Bees and Hive
Stencils 1–2

Stencil 1

Stencil 2

Extra Bee
Stencils 1–2

Stencil 1   Stencil 2

Stencil 1   Stencil 2

47

Springtime Birdhouses Pillow

Finished size: 7" x 8½"

Here's another little pillow to brighten your day. Birdhouses and flowers are a natural combination—choose colors you love and create a garden that lasts all year.

Materials

- 6½" x 7½" piece of blue check fabric for background (I used the wrong side.)
- 1 fat quarter of floral print for borders and pillow back
- 2 pieces of batting, each 10" x 10" (see Tip, page 40)
- Acrylic craft paint in light blue, pink, yellow, white, brown, and green
- Gray, brown, yellow, and green permanent fabric markers (or colors to match your paints)
- ½ yd. of ⅛"-wide purple ribbon
- ½ yd. of ⅛"-wide yellow ribbon
- 8" piece of ½"-wide yellow ribbon
- 1 small brass heart charm
- 4 small clear glass beads
- 2 small snaps
- 1 small flower charm
- 1 small wooden bird
- 1 medium button
- 1 large flower or special button
- Small amount of fiberfill
- Craft glue (optional)

Stenciling

1. Using the pattern on page 51, make a 3-part birdhouse stencil.
2. Center stencil #1 (roofs and trunk) on the background fabric, fuse, and stencil. Use pastels for the roofs, and brown for the trunk and platform.
3. Align stencil #2 with the edges of the roofs and trunk. Fuse. Stencil the houses and chimneys in coordinating light colors. Stencil the flower dots yellow.
4. Align stencil #3 with the edges of the roofs and trunk. Fuse. Stencil the doors and windows in pastels and the leaves in green.
5. Press to heat-set (page 15).
6. Referring to the drawing below and the photograph on the facing page, add outlining and details. Shade the birdhouses with markers of the same color, or use gray on the pastels and brown on the darker colors.

Pen-work details

49

Construction

1. Trim the background ½" from the birdhouse on all sides (pages 18–19).
2. Cut 2"-wide border strips from the floral print. Measure, cut, stitch, and press as described in steps 5–11 on pages 19–20, adding top and bottom borders first. Cut a 10" x 10" square of floral print for the pillow back.
3. Layer the pillow top with 1 piece of batting. Press with a warm iron.
4. Machine quilt in-the-ditch around the border seams (page 21). Hand or machine quilt around the birdhouses.
5. Assemble the pillow as described in steps 7–9 on pages 41–42.

Embellishment

1. Cut a 12" length from the purple ribbon. Make a large, tacked ribbon bow (page 28) and sew to the birdhouse post.
2. Sew a heart charm to the center of the bow knot.
3. Make 5 small rosettes with 4½"-long pieces of the ⅛"-wide yellow ribbon (page 31). Sew rosettes over the yellow painted flower dots, then sew clear beads to the center of each flower.
4. Sew snaps on the small birdhouses and the flower charm on the large white birdhouse.
5. Sew or glue the bird to the white birdhouse.
6. Make a rosette from the ½"-wide yellow ribbon and sew to the bottom right corner with the medium button for the center.
7. Sew the large flower button to the upper left corner.
8. Sign and date the back.

Finishing

Stuff the pillow with fiberfill and whipstitch the opening closed.

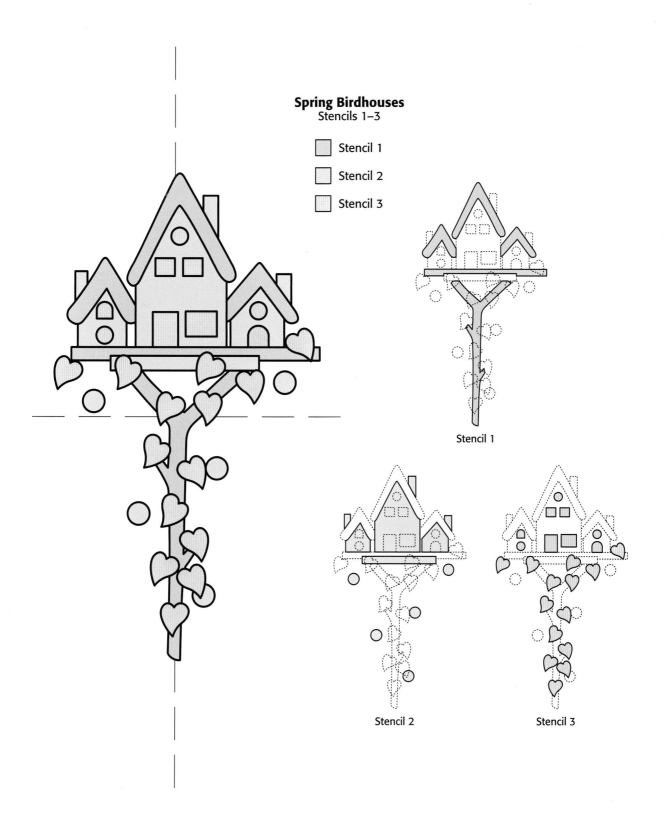

Spring Birdhouses
Stencils 1–3

- ■ Stencil 1
- ▢ Stencil 2
- ▨ Stencil 3

Stencil 1

Stencil 2

Stencil 3

Summer Girl Angel Ornament

Finished size: 4" x 4"

I made this little ornament for a Fourth-of-July decoration in my kitchen. She hangs on a cupboard knob and makes me smile. Choose your favorite holiday and change the colors and lettering to make your own smile starter!

Materials

- 6" x 6" piece of unbleached muslin for background
- 8" x 10" piece of multicolored print fabric for backing, self-binding, and ties
- 6" x 6" square of batting
- Acrylic craft paint in skin color, pink, red, and white
- Gray, brown, and pink permanent fabric markers
- 1 small and 2 medium white buttons
- 4" piece of ¼"-wide red ribbon
- Several multicolored beads
- 1 small trumpet-flower bead
- 3 small red-white-and-blue star sequins and beads or snaps
- 2 medium red-and-blue star sequins and beads
- 1 medium red-and-white button
- Krylon Matte Finish

Stenciling

1. Using the pattern on page 55, make a 3-part angel stencil.
2. Center stencil #1 on the muslin and fuse. Stencil face and feet in skin color and dress in pink. Remove stencil #1.

3. Align stencil #2 with the edges of the face, feet, and dress; fuse. Stencil wings in white. To get the mottled look on the wings, use a large-holed sponge, like a sea sponge or kitchen sponge.
4. Align stencil #3 with the edges of the wings, head, and feet; fuse. Stencil the bodice and underskirt in red, and the banner in white. If necessary, use several thin coats of white to get good coverage.
5. Press to heat-set (page 15).
6. Referring to the drawing below and the photograph on the facing page, add pen-work details. Draw the face as described on pages 27–28. Write "AMERICA" in bold black letters across the banner. Shade the white with a gray marker and the red and pink with a brown marker. Color the cheeks with a pink marker.

Pen-work details

Construction

1. Trim the muslin to 4" x 4½", centering the design.
2. Trim the batting to 4" x 4½". From the multicolored print, cut a 7" x 7" square for the backing.
3. Stack angel, batting, and backing as shown, being sure to center the quilt top and batting on the backing. Press.

4. Hand or machine quilt around the angel figure.
5. Press with a warm iron and trim the backing ½" from the edges of the quilt top all around.

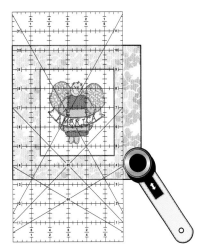

6. Double fold the side edges of the backing over to the front as shown and pin.

Fold.   Fold again
                         and pin.

7. Fold the top and bottom edges to the front in the same manner, square ends, then hand sew the binding to the muslin on all 4 sides. Press.

Embellishment

1. Tear 2 strips of multicolored print, each ½" x 6". Tie the strips together to form one piece, then knot at both ends, leaving ½" tails. Sew the knotted ends to the top corners of the ornament.

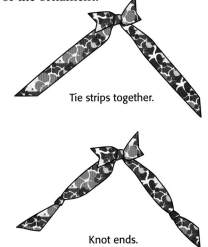

Tie strips together.

Knot ends.

2. Cover the knots with the medium white buttons. Make a red ribbon rosette (page 31) from the ¼"-wide piece of red ribbon. Sew the rosette with a bead center to one, and a string of beads (page 25), ending with the trumpet-flower bead, to the other.

3. Sew small sequins with tiny bead centers on the head, and medium sequins with bead centers to the ends of the banner.

4. Sew a small white button on the dress.

5. Write "Let Freedom Ring" on the red-and-white button with a Sharpie Ultra Fine Point pen (page 27). Let dry 24 hours. Spray with Krylon to set. When dry, sew to the lower right corner with beads in the center.

6. Sign and date your work. Hang your ornament on a cabinet knob and enjoy!

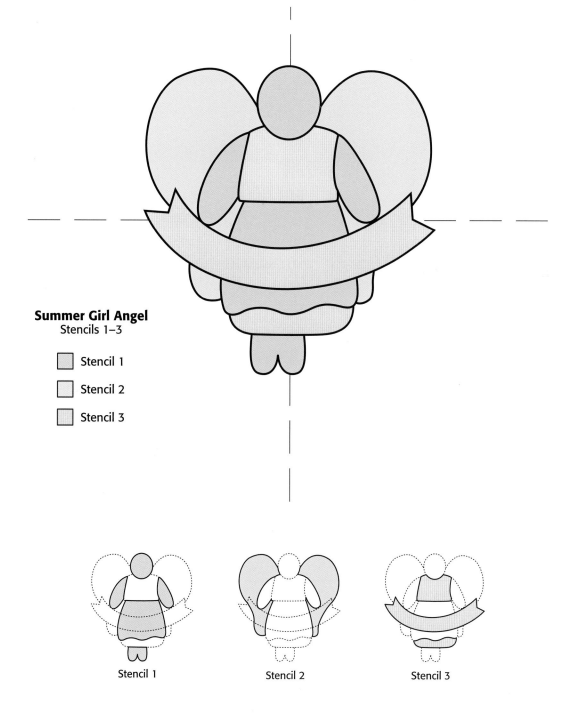

Summer Girl Angel
Stencils 1–3

- ☐ Stencil 1
- ☐ Stencil 2
- ☐ Stencil 3

Stencil 1   Stencil 2   Stencil 3

Fall Pumpkins Pillow

Finished size: 6½" x 7"

For a fall treat, make this plump little pillow in autumn colors and fabrics. It is made the same way as the other pillows, with the addition of contrasting ready-made piping around the edge.

Materials

- 8" x 8" piece of tan fabric for background (try the back of a printed plaid)
- 1 fat quarter of dark teal fabric for border and pillow back
- 2 pieces of batting, each 10" x 10" (see Tip, page 40)
- 1 yd. of tan piping
- Acrylic craft paint in orange, brown, yellow, and green
- Brown permanent fabric marker
- 1" x 22" torn strip of tan polka-dot fabric
- 10" piece of ½"-wide yellow satin ribbon
- 10" piece of ¼"-wide brown ribbon
- 4" piece each of ⅛"-wide and ¼"-wide green ribbon
- 6" piece of ⅛"-wide yellow satin ribbon
- 2 brown buttons
- Approximately 10 assorted beads
- 2 leaf charms
- 1 flower button
- Small amount of fiberfill

Stenciling

1. Using the pattern on page 59, make a 3-part pumpkin stencil.
2. To make 3 different shades of orange, pour 3 puddles of orange paint on a paper plate; add a few drops of brown to one and a few drops of yellow to another. Leave the third as is.
3. Center stencil #1 on the background, fuse, and stencil the pumpkin in 1 shade of orange. Stencil the stems in brown. Remove stencil #1.
4. Align stencil #2 with the edges of the center pumpkin; fuse. Stencil each side pumpkin in a different shade of orange, and the center stem in brown.

5. Align stencil #3 with the pumpkin outlines; fuse. Stencil the leaves in green.
6. Press to heat-set (page 15).
7. Referring to the drawing below and the photograph on the facing page, add pen-work details. Shade with the brown marker.

Pen-work details

Construction

1. Trim the background ½" from the pumpkins on all sides (pages 18–19).
2. Cut 2½"-wide border strips from the dark teal fabric. Measure, cut, stitch, and press as described in steps 5–11 on pages 19–20. Cut a 10" x 10" piece of dark teal fabric for the pillow back.
3. Layer the pillow top with 1 piece of batting. Press with a warm iron.
4. Machine quilt in-the-ditch around the border seams (page 21). Hand or machine quilt around the pumpkins. Press, then trim the batting even with the edges of the pillow top.

5. Starting in the middle of the bottom edge, pin the piping to the right side of the pillow top with raw edges even. Don't try to make the piping square at the corners—just leave a little extra and clip the piping seam allowance at the corners. Cross the ends where they meet at the bottom of the pillow top as shown.

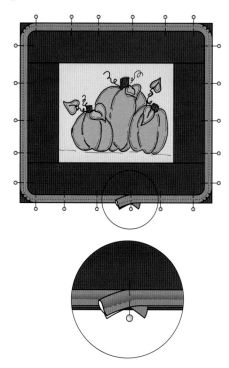

6. Using your zipper foot, sew the piping to the pillow top. Stitch right up next to the cord inside the piping. Stitch straight over the crossed ends as shown.

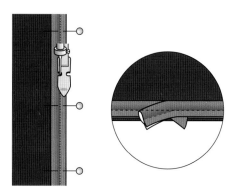

7. Stack the pillow top with the backing and remaining batting piece as shown in the diagram at the bottom of page 41 and pin.
8. With the quilted batting on top, sew around the pillow top right over the stitching done in step 6. Leave a 4" opening for turning.
9. Remove pins, trim corners, and turn right side out.
10. Check to make sure the stitching from step 6 is caught in the seam; restitch any areas where it is not.

Embellishment

Embellish your pillow while you can still put your hand inside to sew.

1. Make a torn-fabric bow (page 29) from the strip of polka-dot fabric, attaching it to the center of the top border.
2. Make concertina roses (page 30) from the ½"-wide yellow ribbon and the ¼"-wide brown ribbon.
3. Form ribbon leaves (page 32) with the green ribbon. Sew the leaves and the yellow and brown roses to the knot on the torn-fabric bow.
4. Cluster the brown buttons, beads, and leaf charms around the roses.
5. Make a rosette (page 31) out of the ⅛"-wide yellow ribbon and a small ribbon leaf from a bit of green ribbon. Sew the rosette with a bead in the center and the leaf onto the stem of the large pumpkin.
6. Sew beads onto other pumpkin stems.
7. Sew the flower button to the lower right corner of the background.

Finishing

Stuff the pillow with fiberfill and whipstitch the opening closed.

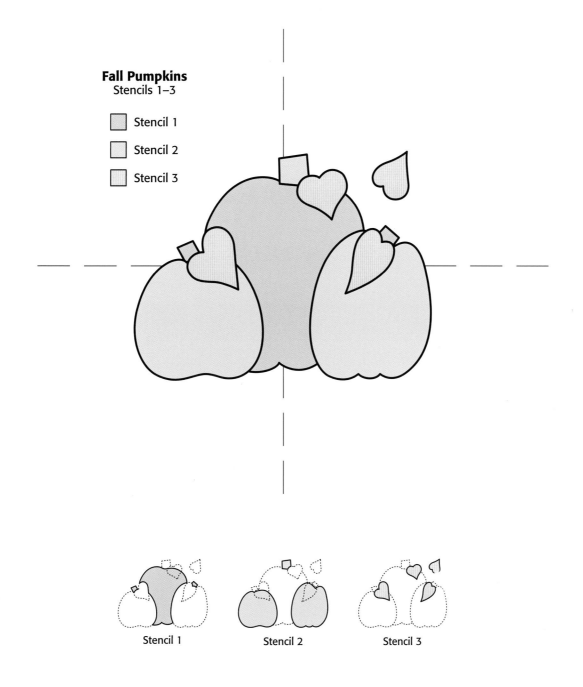

Fall Pumpkins
Stencils 1–3

Stencil 1

Stencil 2

Stencil 3

Stencil 1   Stencil 2   Stencil 3

Cars and Trucks

Finished size: 33½" x 24½"

Even though it's larger, this quilt isn't much more complicated than a mini project. Think of it as making nine little quilts, then sewing them together and adding a border. Easy! And the adorable button faces on the passengers are enough to get anyone motivated.

Materials (44"-wide fabric)

- ⅜ yd. tan fabric for background (I used the same fabric for all the blocks, turning some over for variety. You could also choose up to 9 different background fabrics.)
- 8" x 8" square *each* of 1 red and 1 gold print for sashing
- 10" x 15" piece *each* of 1 blue and 1 green print for sashing
- ⅝ yd. dark blue print for border
- ¼ yd. dark blue stripe for binding
- 1 yd. fabric for backing
- 36" x 27" piece of cotton batting
- Acrylic craft paint in red, blue, white, yellow, green, gray, and black
- Permanent fabric markers in black, gray, pink, yellow, and brown
- Small, medium, and large 2-hole skin-tone buttons
- Krylon Matte Finish
- 10 medium (½" to ¾") and 9 large (1" to 1¼") black buttons (they don't all have to match)
- 2 smaller black-and-white buttons
- Car and truck buttons

Cutting

NOTE: When the directions call for a "crosswise strip" of fabric, use your rotary cutter, ruler, and mat to cut strips the full width of the fabric.

1. From the tan background fabric, cut 9 pieces, each 5" x 8".
2. From the red print, cut 9 pieces, each 1½" x 3½" (vertical sashing). Repeat for the gold print.
3. From the blue print, cut 9 pieces, each 1½" x 8½" (horizontal sashing). Repeat for the green print.
4. From the dark blue print, cut 3 crosswise border strips, each 5" wide.
5. From the dark blue stripe, cut 4 crosswise binding strips, each 2" wide.

Stenciling

1. Using the patterns on pages 64–68, make car and truck stencils.
2. Center car and truck stencils onto the background rectangles and fuse. Referring to the photo on the facing page, use primary paint colors for the car and truck bodies, white for the interiors and headlights, red for the taillights, and gray for the fenders. Paint other elements as desired.
3. Press to heat-set (page 15).
4. Referring to the drawings on page 62 and the photograph on the facing page, add penwork details. Use the names of your favorite school, police department, and fire department. To keep this design childlike, I skipped the squiggle lines and shading, but *never* the outlining!

Block Assembly

1. Trim the background rectangles to 3½" x 6½", centering the designs.

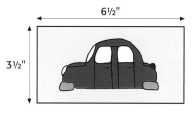

Trim background.

Moving Van

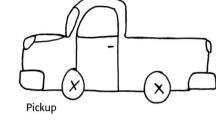

Pickup

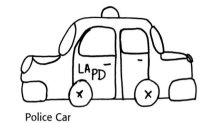

Police Car

SUV

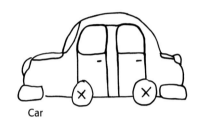

Car

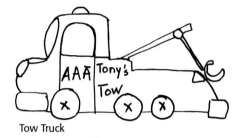

Tow Truck

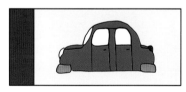

Fire Truck

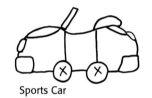

Sports Car

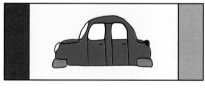

School Bus

Pen-work details

2. Sew a red sashing piece to the left side of each rectangle. Use a consistent seam allowance throughout the project, either ¼" or the width of your presser foot. Press toward the sashing or darker fabric.

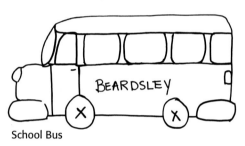

Make 9.

3. Sew a gold sashing piece to the right side of each rectangle. Press toward the sashing or darker fabric.

Make 9.

4. Separate out 6 of the designs: fire truck, moving van, blue car, police car, school bus, and red SUV.

62

5. On each of these rectangles, sew a blue sashing piece to the top and a green sashing piece to the bottom. Press toward the sashing or darker fabric.

Make 6.

6. On the remaining 3 rectangles (pickup, sports car, and tow truck), sew a green sashing piece to the top and a blue sashing piece to the bottom. Press toward the sashing or darker fabric.

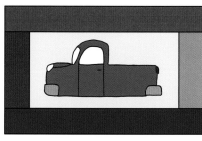

Make 3.

7. If needed, use a rotary cutter, ruler, and mat to square up your finished blocks and trim them all to the same size.

Quilt Top Assembly

1. Lay out your car and truck blocks into 3 vertical rows of 3 blocks each. Join the blocks into rows. Press toward the darker fabric.

2. Join the 3 rows as shown, matching seams. Press toward the darker fabric.

3. Measure, cut, and add the 5"-wide dark blue borders, following steps 5–11 on pages 19–20.

Finishing

Refer to the directions on pages 20–24 to finish your quilt, binding with strips of blue striped fabric.

Embellishment

1. Referring to "Button Faces" on pages 27–28, make 20 button faces. Vary the faces as seen in the photograph on page 60. Add hats, hair, and glasses as desired. Let dry 24 hours, then spray with Krylon. Sew buttons on quilt in vehicle windows.
2. Add black buttons for tires, using the black-and-white buttons for the sports car.
3. Embellish borders with buttons as desired.
4. Sign and date your work.

Cars and Trucks

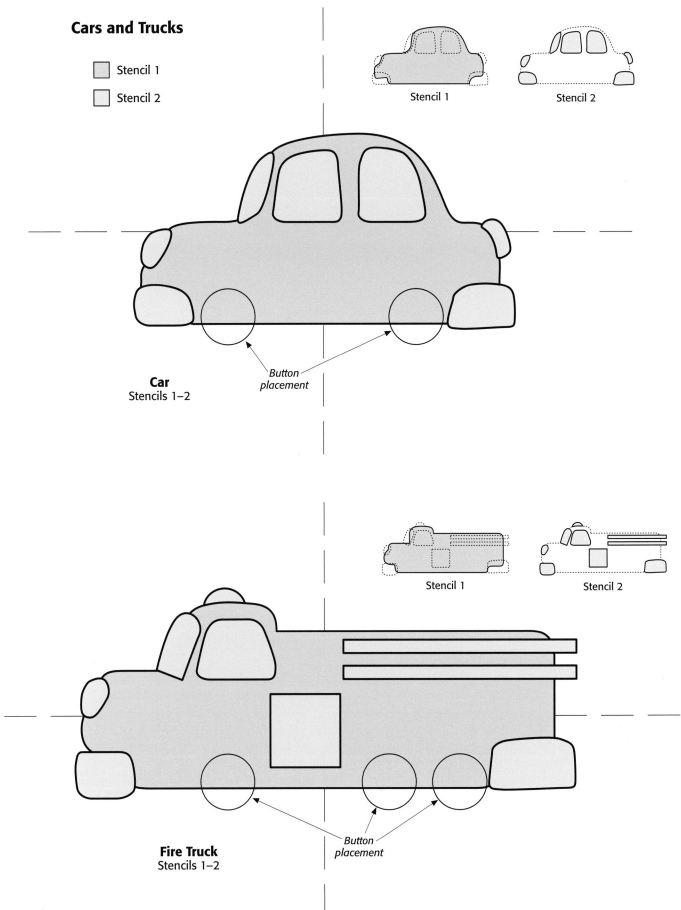

Stencil 1
Stencil 2

Stencil 1   Stencil 2

Car
Stencils 1–2

Button placement

Stencil 1   Stencil 2

Fire Truck
Stencils 1–2

Button placement

Cars and Trucks

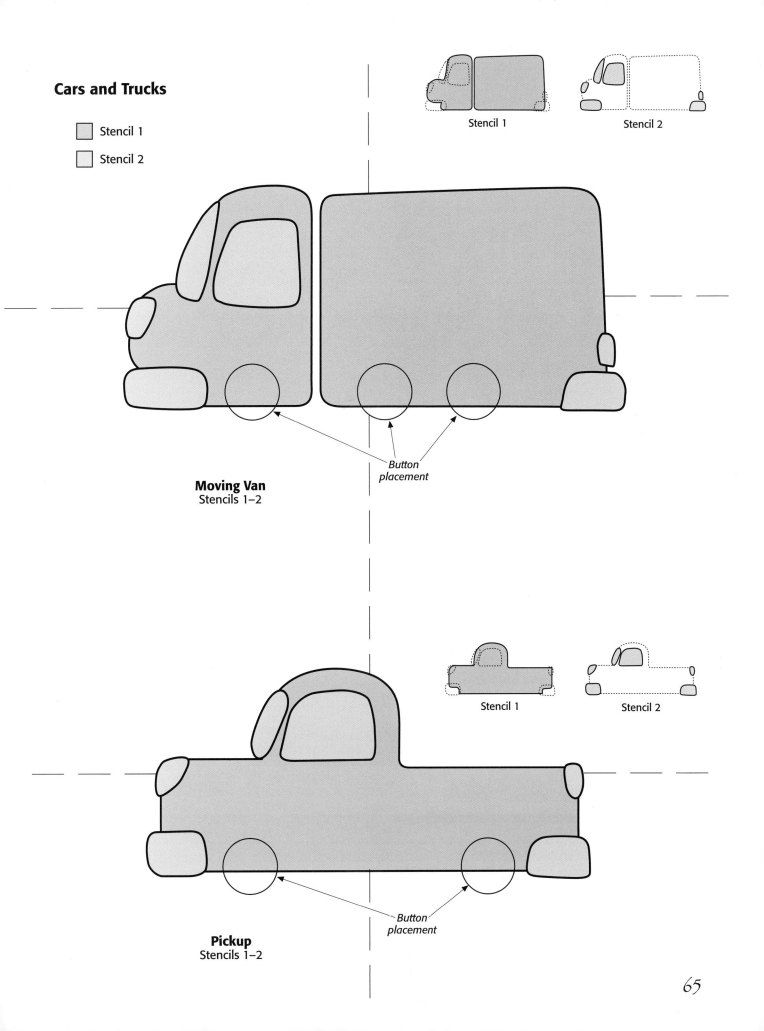

Stencil 1

Stencil 2

Stencil 1

Stencil 2

Moving Van
Stencils 1–2

Button placement

Stencil 1

Stencil 2

Pickup
Stencils 1–2

Button placement

65

Cars and Trucks

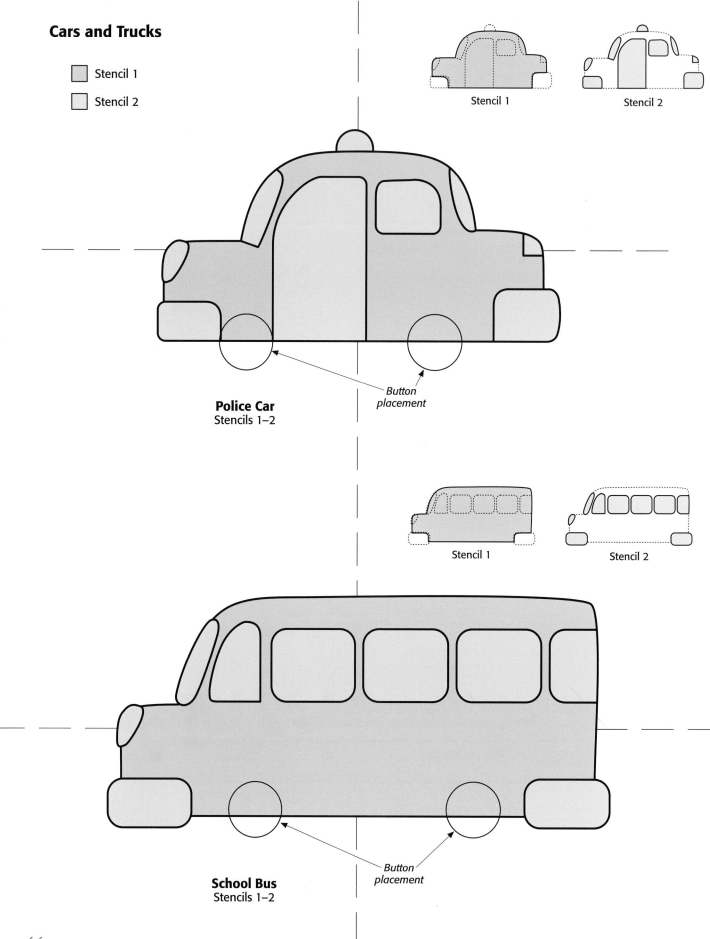

Stencil 1

Stencil 2

Stencil 1

Stencil 2

Stencil 1

Stencil 2

Police Car
Stencils 1–2

Button placement

Stencil 1

Stencil 2

School Bus
Stencils 1–2

Button placement

Cars and Trucks

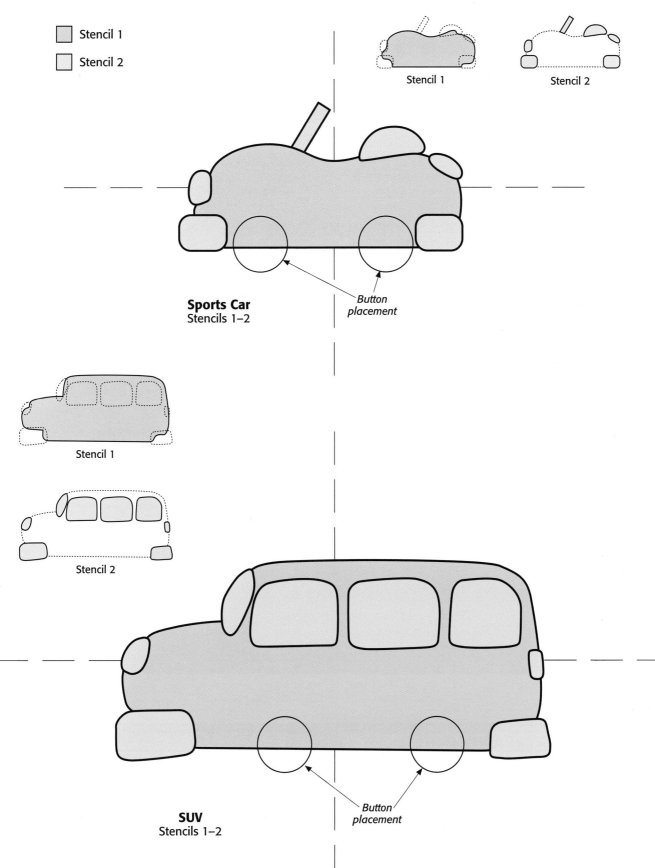

Stencil 1

Stencil 2

Stencil 1

Stencil 2

Sports Car
Stencils 1–2

Button placement

Stencil 1

Stencil 2

SUV
Stencils 1–2

Button placement

Cars and Trucks

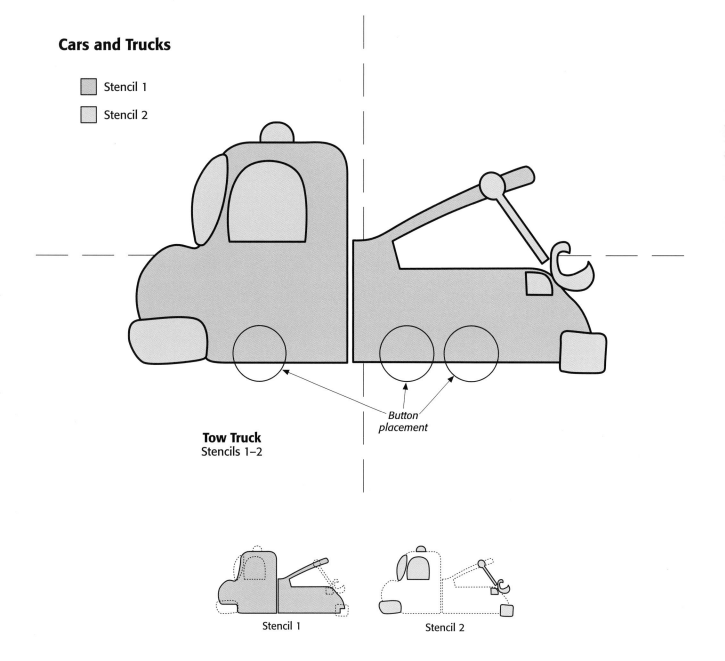

Stencil 1
Stencil 2

Tow Truck
Stencils 1–2

Button placement

Stencil 1   Stencil 2

Stacey's Flower Baskets

Finished size: 31½" x 17"

When I first made this quilt, it rejected the lavender border I put on it. Stacey, my younger son's girlfriend who doesn't sew, picked out the perfect purple print. In honor of her choice, I named the quilt for her.

Materials (44"-wide fabric)

- ⅜ yd. or a 10" x 25" scrap of unbleached muslin for background
- Scraps of 12 assorted light, medium, and dark prints for checkerboard border, each at least 2" x 12"
- ⅞ yd. dark purple print for border and binding
- ⅝ yd. fabric for backing
- 35" x 20" piece of cotton or Warm & Natural batting
- Acrylic craft paint in brown, green, blue, pink, purple, yellow, and white
- Permanent fabric markers in brown and in colors to match paint
- ⅛ yd. light purple print for bow
- ½ yd. *each* of ¼"-wide ribbon in blue, yellow, and purple
- 3" x 3" square *each* of 5 different prints
- 25 assorted buttons (Choose pretty ones that contrast well with your flowers.)
- 3 garden charms

Cutting

NOTE: When the directions call for a "crosswise strip" of fabric, use your rotary cutter, ruler, and mat to cut strips the full width of the fabric.

1. From the muslin, cut 3 squares, each 8" x 8", for stencil backgrounds.
2. From the assorted prints, cut a total of 12 strips, each 1½" x 11".
3. From the dark purple print, cut 3 crosswise strips, each 5" wide, for border and 3 crosswise strips, each 2" wide, for binding.

Stenciling

1. Using the pattern on page 73, make a 4-part flower basket stencil. Make just one of each part, because you will reuse them.
2. Center stencil #1 on a muslin square and fuse. Stencil the basket base and handle in brown. Remove, fuse to a second muslin square, and paint. Repeat for the third muslin square.
3. Align stencil #2 with the edges of the basket and fuse. Paint the leaves green, remove the stencil, and repeat for the remaining 2 squares.
4. Repeat for stencils #3 and #4, varying the flower color placement in the 3 squares.
5. Press to heat-set (page 15).
6. Referring to the drawing below and the photograph on page 69, add pen-work details. The faux buttonhole stitching around the designs simulates folk-art appliqué. Shade leaves and flowers with matching permanent fabric markers and use the brown marker to make the basket weave.

Pen-work details

Quilt Top Assembly

1. Trim the muslin ½" from the bottom of each basket, then trim each square to 6½" x 6½", leaving about the same amount of space on each side of the flowers.

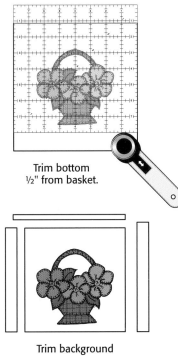

Trim bottom
½" from basket.

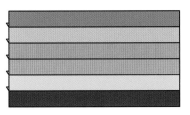

Trim background
to 6½" x 6½",
centering design.

2. Join the 1½" x 11" assorted strips into 2 strip sets of 6 strips each, sewing strips together along the long edges with a ¼"-wide seam. Press all the seam allowances in one direction.

Make 2.

3. Using your rotary cutter, ruler, and mat, trim uneven ends, then crosscut each strip set into 6 segments, each 1½" wide, for a total of 12 segments.

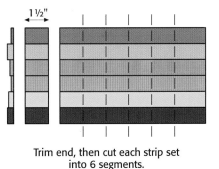

Trim end, then cut each strip set
into 6 segments.

4. Sew a segment to the left side of the left basket square, the right side of the right basket square, and to each side of the center basket square as shown. Press toward the pieced squares. Join the blocks to form a row. Press toward the pieced squares.

Add checkerboard segments, then join blocks.

5. Join the remaining checkerboard segments into 2 long units of 4 segments (24 squares) each. Use your seam ripper to remove 2 squares from the end of each unit. Press.

Join 4 segments end to end, then remove 2 squares.
Make 2.

6. Pin the long units to the top and bottom of the basket row, matching seams at the squares between baskets. Stitch, then press the seam allowances toward the baskets.

7. Cut 2 pieces, each 8½" long, from 1 of the 5"-wide purple border strips. Sew to the sides of the quilt top. Press the seam allowances toward the border.

8. Measure across the quilt top from side to side, including the side borders. Trim the 2 remaining 5"-wide purple border strips to this measurement. Sew to the top and bottom of the quilt and press the seam allowances toward the border.

Finishing

Refer to the directions on pages 20–24 to finish your quilt. Outline-quilt around the baskets and flowers, in-the-ditch at the checkerboard sashing and border seams, and in a diagonal grid in open areas of the basket squares. Bind with the 2"-wide dark purple strips (I used the wrong side of the fabric).

Embellishment

1. Tear the light purple print fabric into 2 strips, each 1½" wide. Tie together and make a couched, torn-fabric bow (page 29). Attach it to the center of the top border.
2. Tie large looped bows of blue, yellow, and purple ribbon. Sew tacked ribbon bows on basket handles as described on pages 28–29.
3. Make 4 assorted folded yo-yos (page 32) and 1 fabric rosette (page 31) from the 3" print squares and sew to the quilt borders.
4. Sew buttons to the centers of the stenciled flowers, yo-yos, and rosette, stacking some (page 25).
5. Sew a cluster of buttons onto the torn-fabric bow knot, and charms onto the ribbon bow knots.
6. With white paint on a dry brush, highlight the buttons and charms with a dab of paint.
7. Sign and date your work.

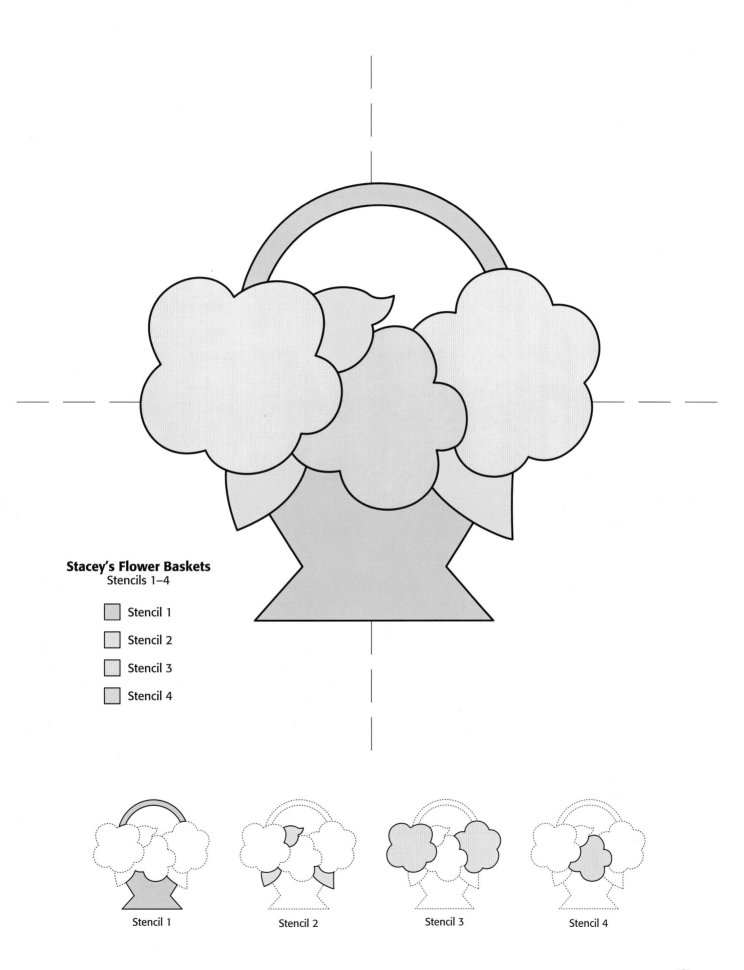

Stacey's Flower Baskets
Stencils 1–4

Stencil 1
Stencil 2
Stencil 3
Stencil 4

Stencil 1

Stencil 2

Stencil 3

Stencil 4

73

Camping in the Woods

Finished size: 29" x 31"

An avid camper, I have been camping and backpacking in the Southern California mountains my whole life.
Written on the quilt are places where I have camped, words from camp songs, and the Girl Scout Pledge.
There are button faces, bugs, wildlife, and fish for my fisherman husband.

Materials (44"-wide fabric)

- ¾ yd. tan print for background (If you want more variety, piece a background to the size given in the directions like I did.)
- ½ yd. blue leaf print for inner border and binding
- ⅝ yd. dark brown print for outer border
- ¼ yd. contrasting blue fabric for bows
- 1 yd. fabric for backing
- 35" x 35" piece of cotton or Warm & Natural batting
- Acrylic craft paint in forest green, brown, tan, blue, yellow, white, red, and black
- Gray and brown permanent fabric markers
- Masking tape
- Krylon Matte Finish
- ½ yd. *each* of ⅛"-wide ribbon in red, dark blue, light blue, and yellow
- 18 small, skin-tone, 2-hole buttons
- 2 large, flat tan buttons
- 22 small and large google eyes
- Craft glue
- Several plastic insects
- 2 small black snaps
- 2 bird buttons
- 2 fish buttons
- 1 small heart button
- 2 flower buttons
- 2 small pearl buttons with shanks
- 1 red and 1 white bead
- 1 glass bead
- 20 assorted buttons
- Charms and beads in a forest motif

Cutting

NOTE: When the directions call for a "crosswise strip" of fabric, use your rotary cutter, ruler, and mat to cut strips the full width of the fabric.

1. From the tan print, cut (or piece) a 19" x 21" background.
2. From the blue leaf print, cut 3 crosswise strips, each 1¾" wide, for inner border; cut 4 crosswise strips, each 2" wide, for binding.
3. From the dark brown print, cut 4 crosswise outer border strips, each 4½" wide.

Stenciling

This is a whole-cloth stenciled quilt. The scene is made up of different motifs combined to build a whole picture. For some of you it will be the easiest quilt to make. Others who like more structure might find it difficult. Jump in and add the things you like best, filling in the spaces until you have a woodland scene you like.

1. Using the patterns on pages 78–81, make cabin, tree, lake, tent, outhouse, animal, fish, sun, campfire, camper, and canoe stencils. Label them carefully so you can keep track! I added a few animal designs, (skunk, fox, etc.) These patterns are not included here, so this is the perfect opportunity to find or create your own stencil patterns!
2. Begin with the cabin stencil. Place the stencil near, but not exactly in, the center of the quilt. Stencil in 2 parts.
3. Stencil the lake in blue in the lower right-hand corner. Paint lightly—you don't need to cover the fabric completely for water, just at the edge.
4. Stencil 4 moose walking across the top of the quilt.
5. Stencil in a couple of large green trees, leaving space between them.

6. To make one object look like it is behind another, such as the tree behind the cabin:
   a. Stencil the forward object first.
   b. Place the stencil for the second object on fabric.
   c. Fuse.
   d. Mask off the painted area with masking tape, freezer paper, or a stick-on note.

Place the tree stencil over the painted cabin.

Mask off the part of the cabin that shows with masking tape, freezer paper, or a stick-on note.

7. Continue to stencil, adding tents, teepees, canoe, animals, etc.
8. After you've added the smaller objects, fill in any large open areas with trees. Stencil the trees at different heights and vary the trunk heights.
9. Press to heat-set (page 15).
10. Referring to the drawings below and the photograph on page 74, add pen-work details. Draw a line from the end of the fishing pole into the lake. Make grass and path with permanent fabric markers and shade as desired. Write favorite camping spots and camp-song verses in open areas around the quilt with a permanent pen. Write the words on paper first, then trace onto fabric. Remember to check for bleeding!

Sun

Bear

Teepee

Tree

Tree

Fish

Moose

Outhouse

Campfire

Pup Tent

Cabin

Pen-work details
For additional pen-work details, refer to the photograph on page 74.

Borders

1. Measure, cut, and add the blue leaf print borders, following steps 5–11 on pages 19–20.
2. Repeat for the dark brown print borders.

Finishing

Refer to the directions on pages 20–24 to finish your quilt. Quilt around your favorite design elements to help them "pop" out. Bind with the 2"-wide blue leaf strips.

Embellishment

1. Using the ⅛"-wide ribbon, make and sew tacked ribbon bows (page 28) around the moose in red, blues, and yellow.
2. Tie knots in 3" lengths of dark and light blue ribbon and sew to the bears, meandering the ribbon tails.
3. Make 18 button faces (pages 27–28) in different colors and sizes. Give some hair and some hats. Let dry 24 hours, then spray with Krylon. Sew onto tents, teepee, cabin, and canoe.

4. Using the Ultra Fine Point Sharpie, draw a compass on 1 large tan button. Write your quilt's title on the other large tan button (page 27). Spray with Krylon when dry. Sew the buttons to the quilt.

5. Glue google eyes to trees; sew on insects.
6. Sew small snaps onto trailer for tires.
7. Sew bird buttons in sky, fish buttons in lake, heart button on door, flower buttons around cabin, pearl buttons for marshmallows over fire, and red and white beads on fishing line. Sew on glass beads for doorknobs on cabin and outhouse.
8. From the contrasting blue fabric, tear 2 crosswise strips, each 2" wide, and 1 crosswise strip, 1½" wide. Tie the 2" strips together and make a big, loopy bow. Try to hide the knot that joins the strips in the bow knot. Tie a single loop in the 1½"-wide strip.
9. Make torn-fabric bows (page 29) at top left (double loop) and bottom right (single loop). Sew buttons onto bow knots and loops and scatter more around the quilt, layering them with other buttons and beads. Add charms and beads as desired.
10. Sign and date your work.

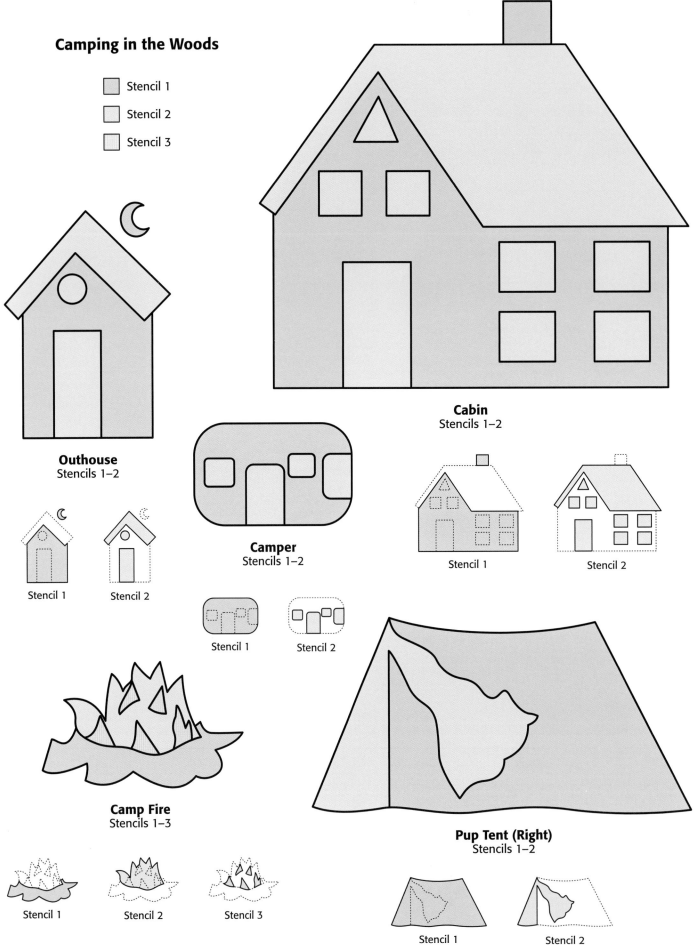

Camping in the Woods

Stencil 1
Stencil 2
Stencil 3

Outhouse
Stencils 1–2

Stencil 1   Stencil 2

Camper
Stencils 1–2

Stencil 1   Stencil 2

Cabin
Stencils 1–2

Stencil 1   Stencil 2

Camp Fire
Stencils 1–3

Stencil 1   Stencil 2   Stencil 3

Pup Tent (Right)
Stencils 1–2

Stencil 1   Stencil 2

Camping in the Woods

■ Stencil 1
□ Stencil 2

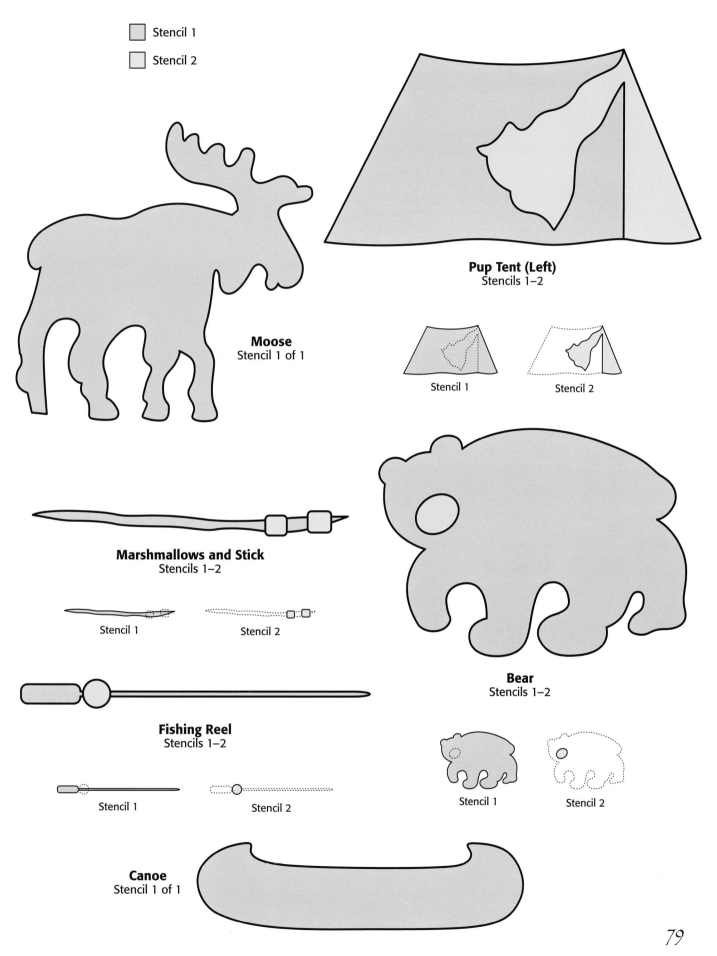

Moose
Stencil 1 of 1

Pup Tent (Left)
Stencils 1–2

Stencil 1　　Stencil 2

Marshmallows and Stick
Stencils 1–2

Stencil 1　　Stencil 2

Bear
Stencils 1–2

Fishing Reel
Stencils 1–2

Stencil 1　　Stencil 2

Stencil 1　　Stencil 2

Canoe
Stencil 1 of 1

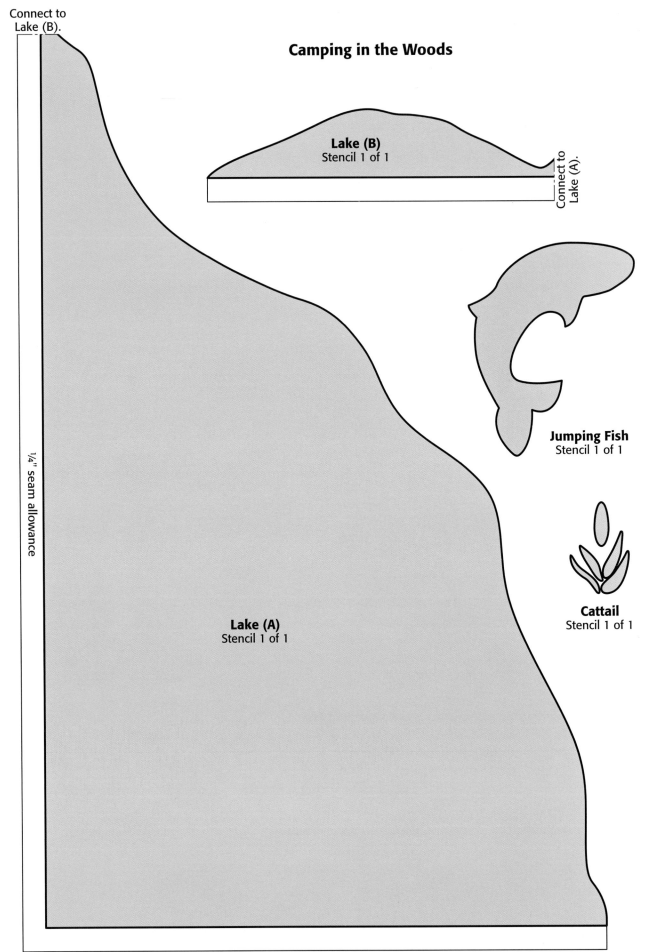

Camping in the Woods

Lake (B)
Stencil 1 of 1

Connect to Lake (A).

Connect to Lake (B).

¼" seam allowance

Jumping Fish
Stencil 1 of 1

Cattail
Stencil 1 of 1

Lake (A)
Stencil 1 of 1

Camping in the Woods

Tepee
Stencil 1 of 1

Sun
Stencil 1 of 1

Tiny Tree
Stencil 1 of 1

Medium Tree
Stencil 1 of 1

Small Tree
Stencil 1 of 1

Large Tree
Stencil 1 of 1

Rose of Sharon

Finished size: 38" x 38"

Stenciled quilts were made in New England from 1830–1860, but little is known about them today. Only thirty of these antique quilts remain for us to study. This easy stenciled quilt is a tribute to our foremothers who took paint to fabric and made very different quilts for their day.

Materials (44"-wide fabric)

- 2 yds. muslin for stenciled blocks, middle border, and backing (muslin was a common backing fabric for stenciled quilts)
- 1 yd. large-scale brown floral print for alternate squares, outer border, and binding
- ¼ yd. red-brown print for inner border
- 45" x 45" piece of batting
- Acrylic craft paint in rose, dark rose, and green
- Masking tape
- 13 medium ivory buttons (old mother-of-pearl buttons are perfect)

Cutting

NOTE: When the directions call for a "cross-wise strip" of fabric, use your rotary cutter, ruler, and mat to cut strips the full width of the fabric.

1. From the muslin, first cut a 42" x 42" square for the backing, then cut 5 squares, each 6½" x 6½", and 3 crosswise border strips, each 4½" wide.
2. From the brown floral print, cut 4 squares, each 6½" x 6½"; 4 crosswise border strips, each 5½" wide; and 4 crosswise binding strips, each 2" wide.
3. From the red-brown print, cut 4 crosswise border strips, each 1½" wide.

Quilt Top Assembly

Make the quilt top, then stencil everything at once.

1. Sew the 6½" muslin and brown floral print squares into rows. Press toward the print. Join the rows. Press the seam allowances in one direction.

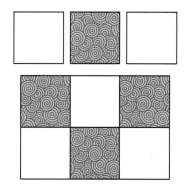

2. Measure, cut, and add the 1½"-wide red-brown inner borders, following steps 5–11 on pages 19–20.
3. Repeat for the 4½"-wide muslin borders and the 5½"-wide brown floral borders.

Stenciling

1. Using the patterns on pages 86–89, make a 2-part rose stencil and a 2-part border stencil. To make the border stencil:
   a. Cut 2 pieces of freezer paper, each 4½" x 17". Tape them together with masking tape to form an L. Trim as shown.

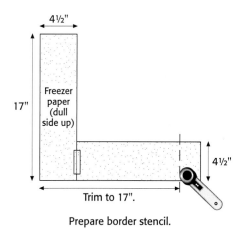

Prepare border stencil.

b. Starting with the corner rose, trace the design onto the freezer paper, joining patterns where indicated. Place the inner edge of your freezer-paper L along the dashed lines on the pattern.

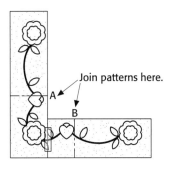

c. Repeat for rose border stencil #2.

2. Crease the quilt center in an X from corner to corner. Next, crease the corner muslin squares perpendicular to the previous creases. All 5 muslin squares should now have 2 diagonal creases running through their centers.

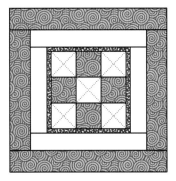

Crease muslin squares on the diagonal.

3. Stencil a Rose of Sharon in the exact middle of each muslin block. Use rose paint for the large outer petals and bud tips, dark rose for the smaller inner petals, and green for the leaves.

4. To stencil the borders:

    a. Find the center of each muslin border. Pin to mark.

    b. Position rose border stencil #1 on the fabric with the corner rose in the corner, the middle of each center rose at a pin mark, and the inner edge of the freezer paper along the inner border seam.

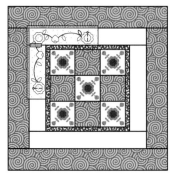

Position stencil on border.

    c. If the stencil is too long, take a little tuck in it before you fuse. If it is too short, cut across the middle of a vine, then use masking tape to bridge the gap.

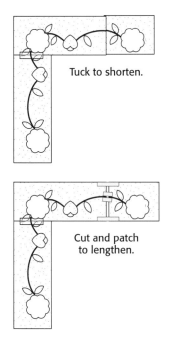

Tuck to shorten.

Cut and patch to lengthen.

d. Fuse, then begin stenciling in the corners, using the same paint colors you used for the blocks.

e. Peel off stencil #1 and move to the next corner. Position, following steps b and c. One of your center roses should line up perfectly with a painted center rose. Fuse and paint. Repeat on the next 2 corners. On the last corner, you won't need to paint any center roses.

f. Repeat for rose border stencil #2.

5. Press the entire quilt to heat-set (page 15).

6. Referring to the drawings below and the photograph on page 82, add pen-work details with the Sharpie pen (check for bleeding first).

Finishing

1. Refer to the directions on pages 20–24 to finish your quilt, binding with the 2"-wide brown floral strips. For an antique look, quilt around the flowers and leaves, then on the diagonal across the quilt.

2. Stitch an ivory button to the center of each rose.

3. Sign and date your new "antique" stenciled quilt and spread the word about antique stenciled quilts!

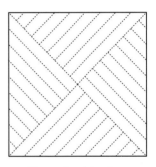

Diagonal quilting lines

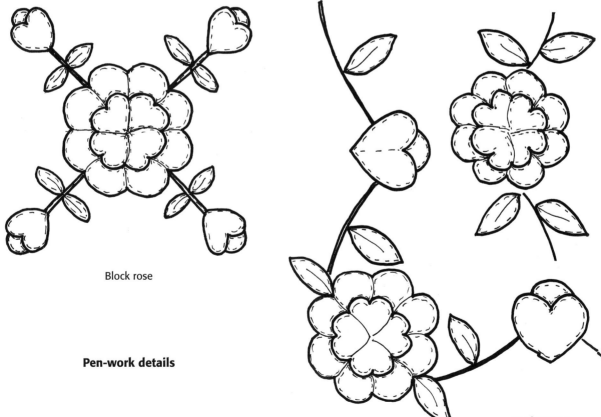

Block rose

Pen-work details

Border roses

85

Rose of Sharon

Rose Block
Stencils 1–2

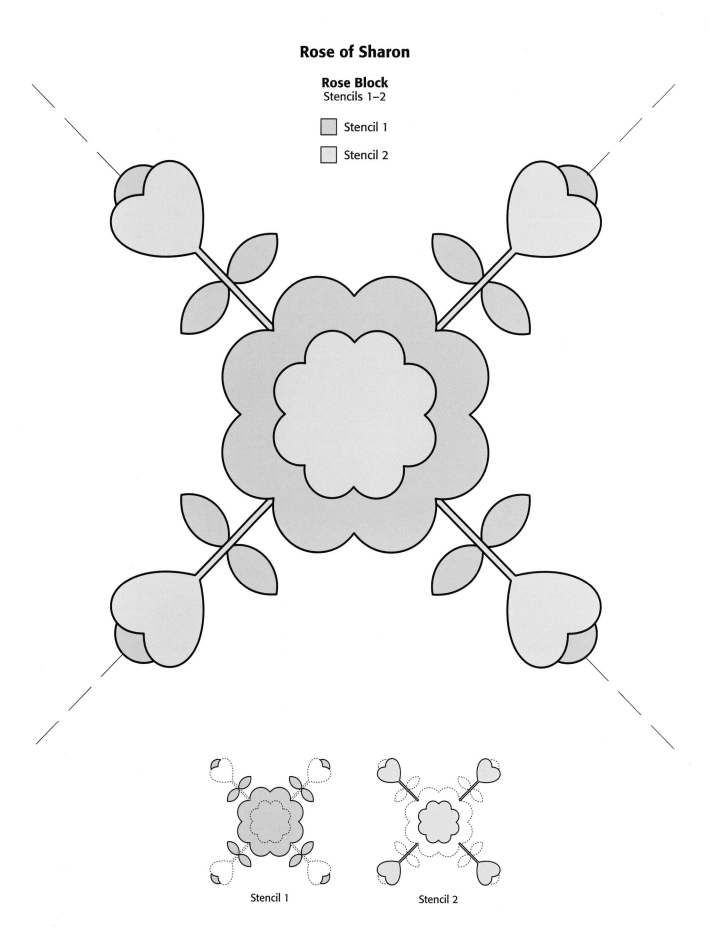

Stencil 1

Stencil 2

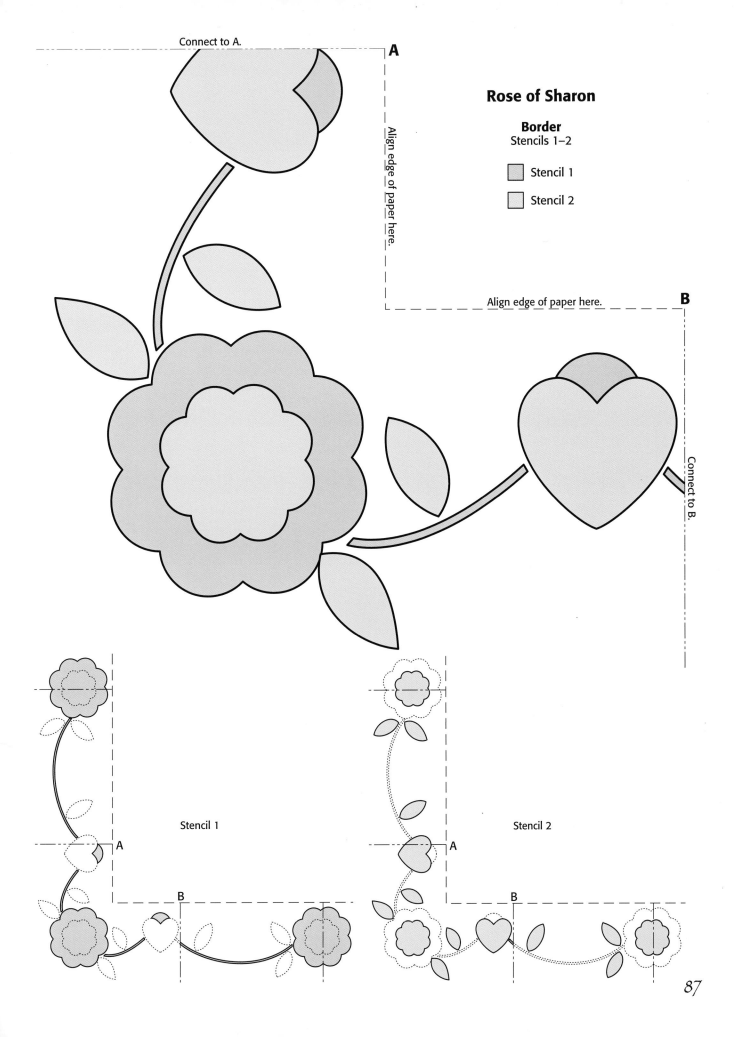

Connect to A.

A

Align edge of paper here.

Rose of Sharon

Border
Stencils 1–2

Stencil 1

Stencil 2

Align edge of paper here.

B

Connect to B.

Stencil 1

A

B

Stencil 2

A

B

87

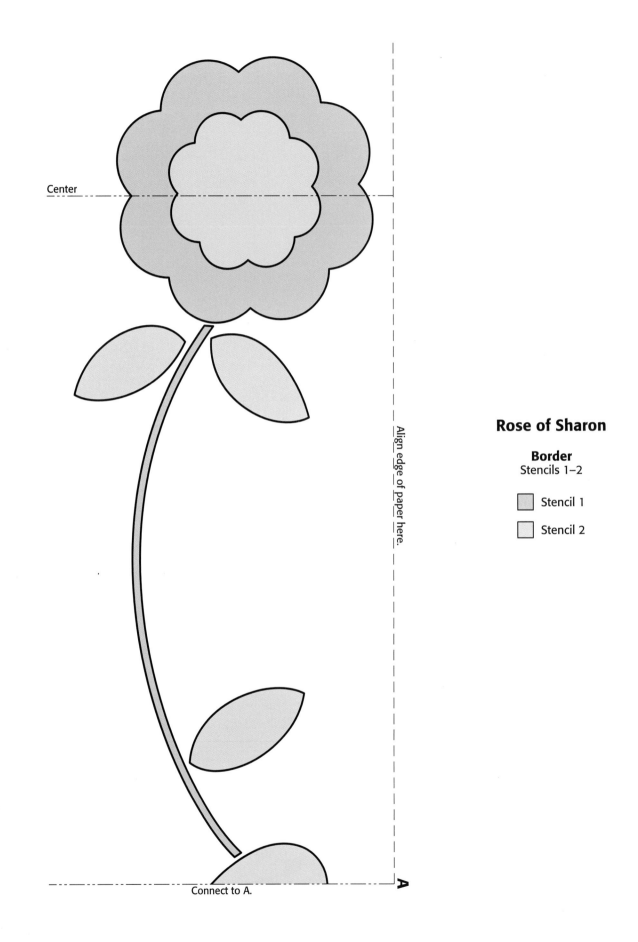

Center

Align edge of paper here.

Connect to A.

A

Rose of Sharon

Border
Stencils 1–2

Stencil 1

Stencil 2

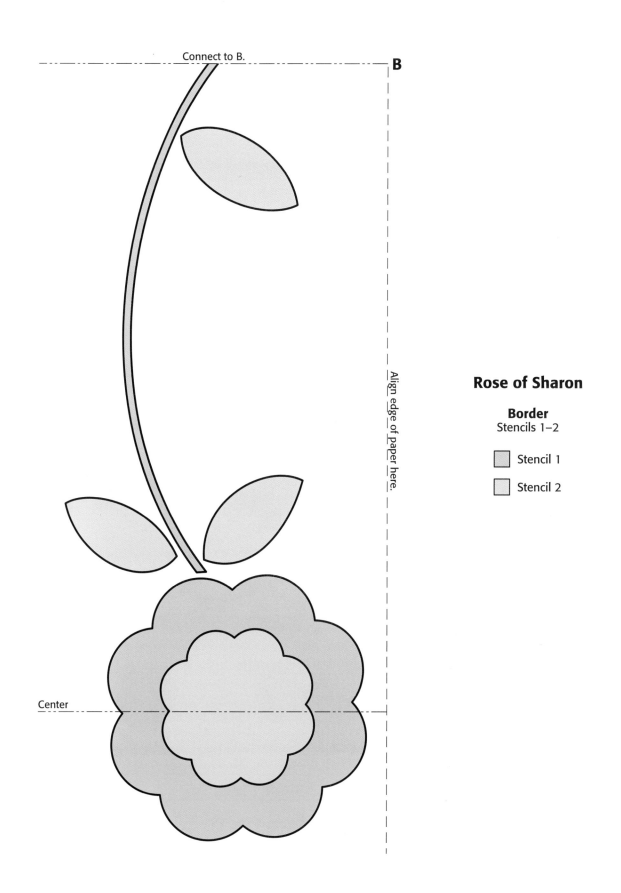

Connect to B.

B

Align edge of paper here.

Center

Rose of Sharon

Border
Stencils 1–2

Stencil 1

Stencil 2

Bees and Bears

Finished size: 35" x 35"

Bears and bees just go together. The Bee blocks are based on a traditional block with a nine-patch center and appliquéd bees in the corners. Bear and Four Patch blocks, a central hive, and bright red flowers complete the scene.

Materials (44"-wide fabric)

- 1½ yds. muslin for background, four- and nine-patch squares, and stenciled border
- ⅜ yd. deep red print for four- and nine-patch squares and inner border
- ⅜ yd. rose solid for binding
- 1¼ yds. fabric for backing
- 40" x 40" piece of batting
- Acrylic craft paint in red, gold, yellow, brown, tan, black, and white
- Masking tape
- Permanent fabric markers in pink and gold
- 16 medium brown buttons
- 1 yd. of ¼"-wide red ribbon
- 1 yd. of ⅛"-wide red ribbon
- ½ yd. of ⅛"-wide green ribbon
- 1 small white button
- 1 large and 1 small bead

Cutting

NOTE: When the directions call for a "crosswise strip" of fabric, use your rotary cutter, ruler, and mat to cut strips the full width of the fabric.

1. From the muslin, cut:
   4 squares, each 5½" x 5½"
   18 pieces, each 2½" x 3½"
   8 pieces, each 2½" x 7½"
   1 piece, 3½" x 7½"
   3 crosswise strips, each 1½" wide. From 1 strip, cut 1 piece, 14" long, 2 pieces, each 7" long, and 1 piece, 10" long.
   4 crosswise strips, each 6½" wide, for outer border
2. From the deep red print, cut 7 crosswise strips, each 1½" wide. From 1 strip, cut 2 pieces, each 14" long, and 1 piece, 7" long. From a second strip, cut a 10" piece.
3. From the rose solid, cut 4 crosswise strips, each 2" wide, for binding.

Stenciling: Part One

Stencil the bears first, then stencil the bees and hive after the quilt top is assembled.

1. Using the patterns on pages 95–99, make a 3-part bear stencil, a 2-part beehive stencil, a 2-part bee stencil, and a pieced 2-part border stencil. For the border stencil, follow the directions on pages 83–84. For each stencil, cut 1 freezer-paper strip 5" x 20" and another 5" x 9". Tape them together to form an L and trace.

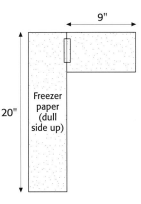

NOTE: Make at least 3 of each bee stencil, because you will be using each one 16 times.

2. Use a pencil or water-soluble marker to draw ¼" seam-allowance lines along 2 adjoining edges of each 5½" muslin square. Mark lightly.

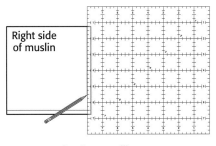

Mark ¼" seam alllowances.

3. Place bear stencil #1 on a 5½" muslin square, aligning the straight edges of the stencil opening with the seam-allowance lines you marked in the last step. Fuse and stencil in brown. Remove and repeat on the remaining muslin squares.

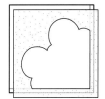

4. Continue with stencils #2 and #3, lining up the bear's ears and the seam-allowance lines. Stencil the muzzle in tan and the eyes and nose in black. Save the bear paws and pen work for later.

Unit Assembly

Nine-Patch Units

1. Using the 1½" x 14" and 1½" x 7" muslin and red pieces, sew the pieces into strip sets as shown, sewing strips together along the long edges with a ¼"-wide seam. Press the seam allowances toward the red.

14"

Make 1.

7"

Make 1.

2. Trim the ends, then crosscut the strip sets into 1½"-wide segments as shown.

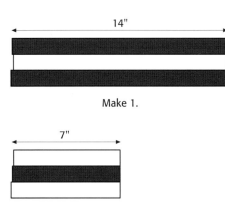

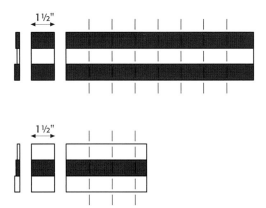

3. Make 4 dark nine-patch units.

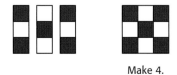

Make 4.

Four-Patch Units

1. Using the 1½" x 10" muslin and red pieces, along with 1 whole crosswise strip of each fabric, sew the pieces into strip sets as shown, sewing strips together along the long edges with a ¼"-wide seam. Press the seam allowances toward the red.

10"

Make 1.

42"

Make 1.

2. Trim the ends, then crosscut the strip sets into 1½"-wide segments as shown.

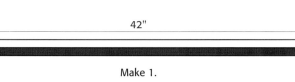

1½"

1½"

3. Make 16 four-patch units.

Make 16.

Block and Quilt Top Assembly

1. Join four-patch units and 2½" x 3½" pieces as shown.

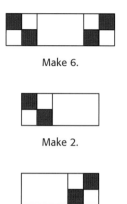

Make 6.

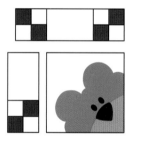

Make 2.

Make 2.

2. Lay out 4 Bear blocks, using the stenciled squares and units made in step 1. Refer to the photo and diagram for four-patch placement.

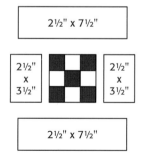

Make 2.   Make 2.

3. Assemble the blocks. Press.

4. Lay out and assemble the Bee blocks, using nine-patch units, 2½" x 3½" muslin pieces, and 2½" x 7½" muslin pieces. Press.

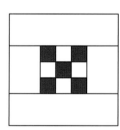

Bee Block
Make 4.

5. Lay out and assemble 1 Beehive block, using the 3½" x 7½" muslin piece and the remaining four-patch units from step 1. Press.

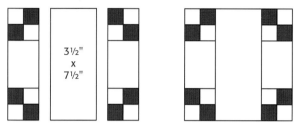

Make 1.

6. Arrange the blocks into 3 rows of 3 blocks each. Stitch the blocks into rows. Press toward the Bear blocks (top and bottom rows) and Beehive block (center row). Join the rows. Press the seam allowances up.

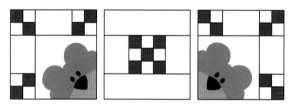
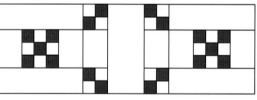
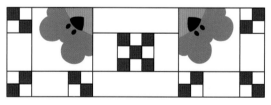

7. Measure, cut, and add an inner border of 1½"-wide red print strips, following steps 5–11 on pages 19–20.

8. Add a 6½"-wide muslin border in the same manner.

Stenciling: Part Two

1. Position beehive stencil #1 in the middle of the center block. Fuse and stencil in gold. Stencil the door in brown.
2. Place bees in the corners of the Bee blocks. Stencil the body in gold, wings in white, and stripes in black. It's okay if bees overlap blocks a little.
3. Stencil a bear's paw on each Bear block, overlapping the nearest Bee block.
4. To stencil the borders:

   a. Position border stencil #1 in one corner so that the inner edge of the freezer paper lines up with the inner border seam. Fuse. Stencil the 4 flowers.

   b. Peel off the stencil and move it around to the next corner. Fuse and paint. Repeat for the remaining 2 corners.

   c. Apply stencil #2 in the same manner, taking care to line up the vine sections at "C" each time you move to a new corner.
5. Press the entire quilt to heat-set (page 15).
6. Referring to the drawings below and the photograph on page 90, add pen-work

details. Shade beehive with gold marker around door and edges. Shade bears' cheeks and ears with pink. Dip a toothpick in white paint and dot each bear's eyes and nose. Outline flowers, leaves, and vine.

Finishing

Refer to the directions on pages 20–24 to finish your quilt. Outline-quilt around the bears, bees, beehive, and flowers, then quilt diagonally through the Four-Patch blocks. Bind with the 2"-wide rose strips.

Embellishment

1. Sew brown buttons in stenciled flowers a little off-center.
2. Make 2 rosettes of ¼"-wide red ribbon, 1 of ⅛"-wide red ribbon, and ribbon leaves of green ribbon (pages 31–32). Sew in a cluster over the beehive door with button and beads in flower centers.
3. Make and sew a tacked ribbon bow (page 28) of ⅛"-wide red ribbon on hive top.
4. Sign and date your work.

Pen-work details

Hive

Bear

Bee

Border

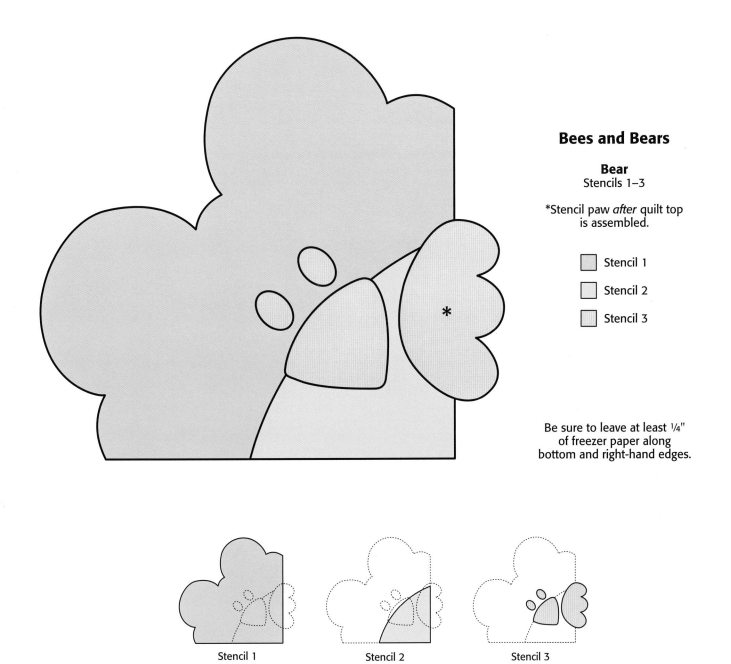

Bees and Bears

Bear
Stencils 1–3

*Stencil paw *after* quilt top is assembled.

	Stencil 1
	Stencil 2
	Stencil 3

Be sure to leave at least ¼" of freezer paper along bottom and right-hand edges.

Stencil 1

Stencil 2

Stencil 3

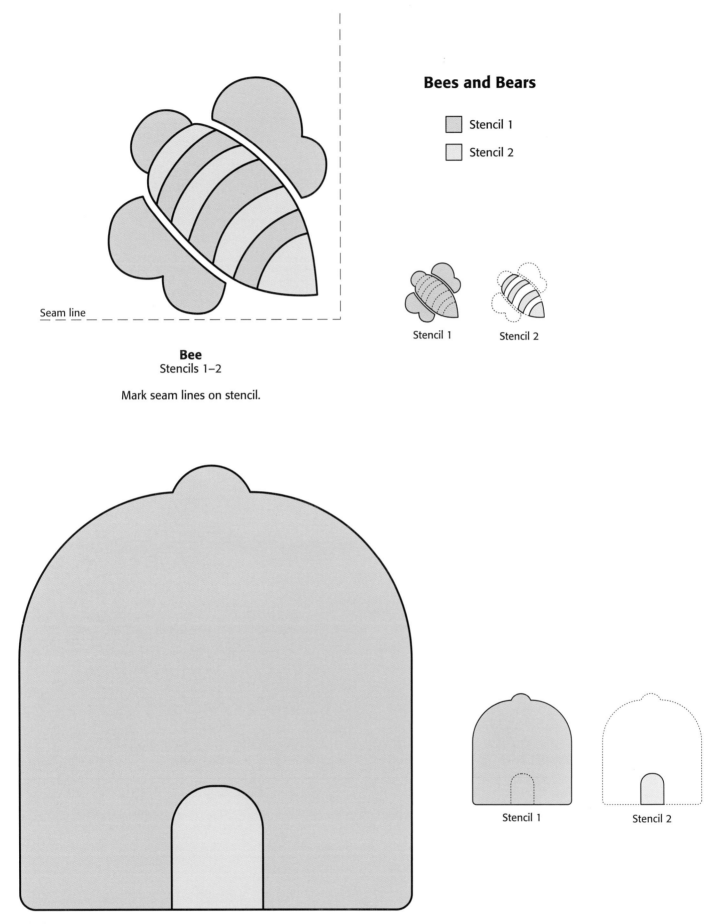

Bees and Bears

Stencil 1

Stencil 2

Seam line

Bee
Stencils 1–2

Mark seam lines on stencil.

Stencil 1   Stencil 2

Bee Hive
Stencils 1–2

Stencil 1   Stencil 2

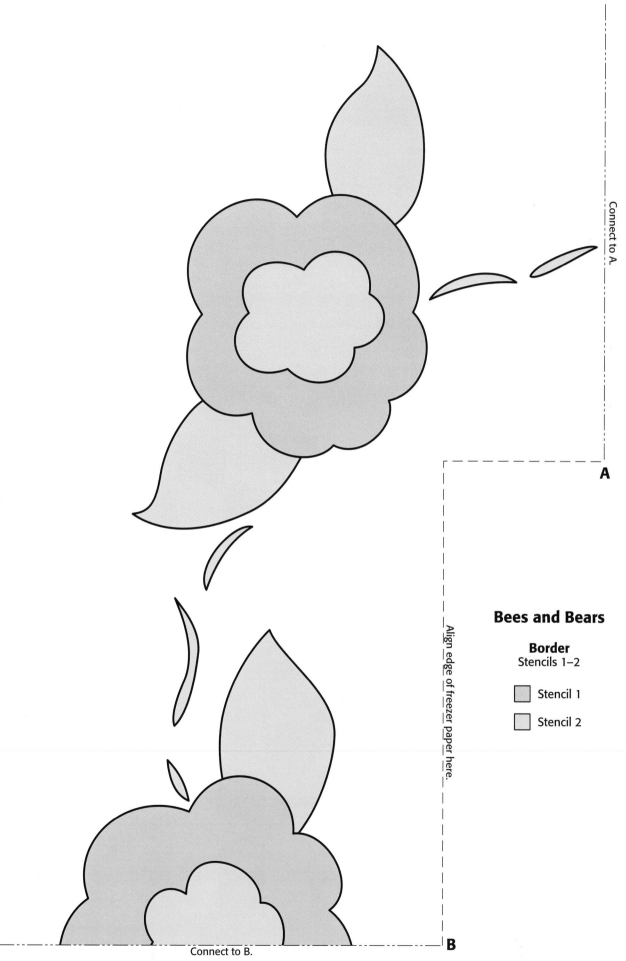

Connect to A.

A

Align edge of freezer paper here.

Bees and Bears

Border
Stencils 1–2

Stencil 1

Stencil 2

B

Connect to B.

97

Connect to B.

B

Align edge of freezer paper here.

Bees and Bears

Border
Stencils 1–2

Stencil 1

Stencil 2

C

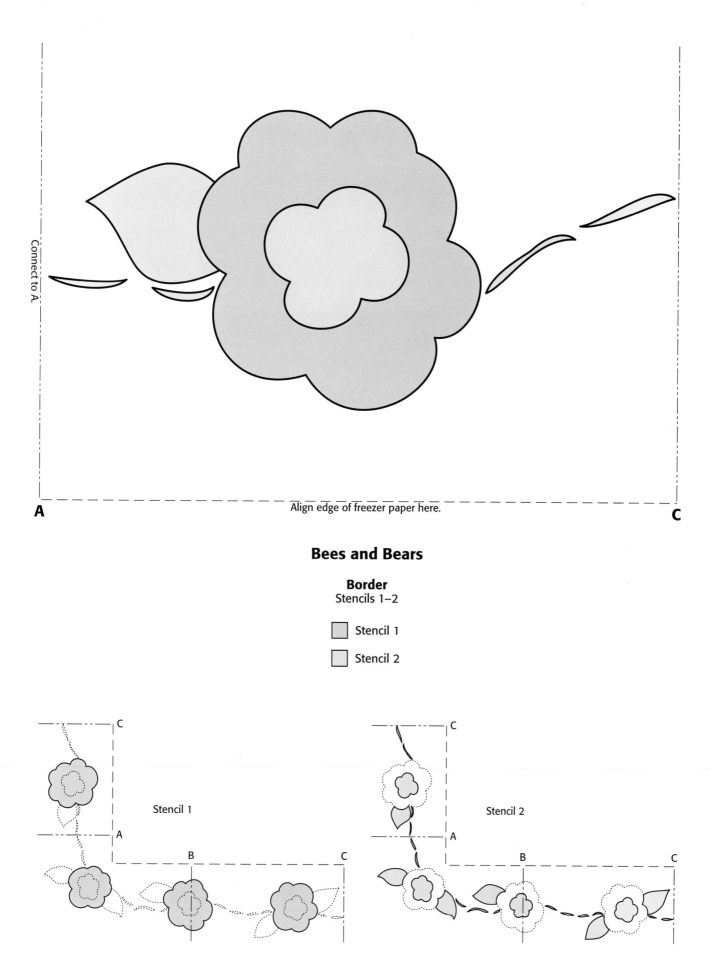

Connect to A.

A   Align edge of freezer paper here.   C

Bees and Bears

Border
Stencils 1–2

Stencil 1

Stencil 2

C

A

Stencil 1

B   C

C

A

Stencil 2

B   C

Town Squared

Finished size: 43" x 43"

Four seasons in the life of an adorable town surround vibrant Nine Patch blocks. I recommend making the quilt first, then stenciling the border so the stenciled town fits perfectly.

Materials (44"-wide fabric)

- 8" x 14" scrap *each* of 12 different prints in dark and medium tones for the nine-patch squares (I used one dark and one medium print each of red, blue, yellow, green, purple, and black.)
- 2 yds. unbleached muslin for the nine-patch squares and stenciled border (For a scrappy look, choose several fat quarters (1 yd. total) of light prints for the patchwork and 1 yd. of unbleached muslin for the border.)*
- ⅝ yd. dark green print for inner border and binding
- 1⅜ yds. of 60"-wide fabric for backing
- 50" x 50" piece of batting
- Acrylic craft paint in white and green plus a wide range of light to dark shades that coordinate with your nine-patch fabric colors—choose about 15 shades in all
- Permanent fabric markers in colors to match your paints
- Embellishments: various ribbons, beads, buttons, charms, and trims

* Muslin must be unbleached for white paint to show up.

Cutting

NOTE: When the directions call for a "cross-wise strip" of fabric, use your rotary cutter, ruler, and mat to cut strips the full width of the fabric.

1. Slice your print scraps into 2" x 12" strips (about 3 per fabric).
2. From the muslin, cut:
   12 crosswise strips, each 2" wide; cut each strip into 12" pieces
   4 crosswise strips, each 7" wide (stenciled border)
   2 pieces, each 4" x 7", for piecing border (Omit if your muslin measures at least 43" wide after you trim the selvages and preshrink.)
3. From the dark green print, cut 4 crosswise strips, each 2" wide, for inner border. Cut 4 crosswise strips, each 2" wide, and 2 pieces, each 2" x 6", for binding. The 6" pieces can be cut from the inner border strips.

Nine Patch Blocks

1. Sew your 2" x 12" muslin and print strips into strip sets as shown, sewing strips together along the long edges with a ¼"-wide seam. Use the same fabric for both print strips in each dark set, then make a light set with that fabric as well. Press all the seam allowances toward the print.

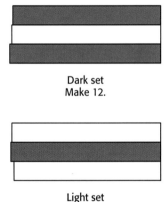

Dark set
Make 12.

Light set
Make 12.

2. Trim the uneven ends, then crosscut the strip sets into 2" segments as shown.

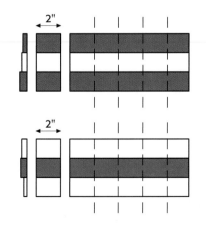

3. Join the segments to make 18 dark Nine Patch blocks and 18 light Nine Patch blocks, including some mismatched ones. You will have several segments left over. Press toward the dark segments.

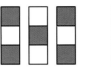

Dark Nine Patch
Make 18.

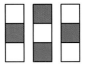

Light Nine Patch
Make 18.

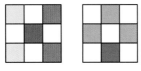

Mismatched blocks

Quilt Top Assembly

1. Lay out the Nine Patch blocks in 6 rows of 6 blocks each, alternating dark and light blocks. Join the blocks to form rows. Press the seam allowances in alternate directions from row to row. Join the rows. Press the seam allowances up.

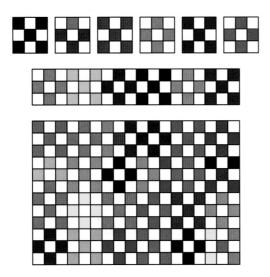

2. Measure, cut, and add the dark green print borders, following steps 5–11 on pages 19–20.
3. If your muslin measures less than 43" across, sew the 4" x 7" muslin pieces to 2 muslin border strips to lengthen (top and bottom borders). Press the seams open.
4. Add muslin borders in the same way.

Stenciling

1. Using the patterns on pages 107–110, make building and tree stencils. Be sure to label them to help you keep track.
2. Fold the quilt top in half twice to make a crease in the center of each muslin border. This crease is the beginning point for building your stenciled town.
3. Start with one side of the quilt. Pick a season and select paint colors that reflect that season. Check the painting tips on the facing page before you begin. Choose a favorite feature, like the school, and iron stencil #1 to the muslin border. I like things a little off-center, so I would place it to one side of the crease. For a symmetrical border, center the building at the crease. Be sure to place the bottom of the building close to the edge of the green border.

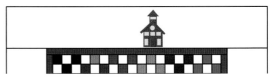

Asymmetrical placement

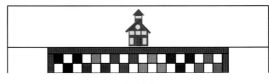

Symmetrical placement

4. Stencil the building in the proper sequence.

5. Add buildings until you have 4 or 5 assorted buildings on the border. Alternate tall and short buildings and leave room for trees and bushes in between.

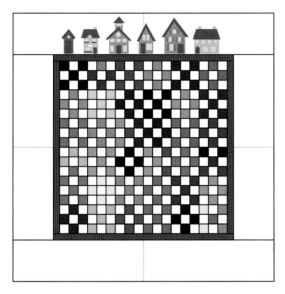

6. Turn the quilt and stencil the next season in new colors on the adjoining border. Don't worry about making the borders match. Repeat for the remaining 2 borders.

7. Add trees to all the borders at once, using a different color scheme for each season. Be sure to use the technique described in step 6 on page 76 to create the illusion that some trees and bushes are behind buildings.

8. Stencil trees in the corners, placing them on the diagonal.

Painting Tips

Include seasonal accents like a Christmas tree for the winter scene, red and gold leaves in the fall scene, etc.

• Stencil the winter roofs in white. After you finish stenciling the buildings, dip a toothpick or pin in white paint and add icicles to the roof lines.

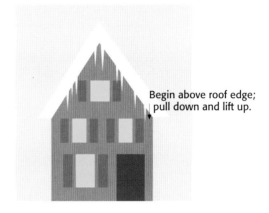

Begin above roof edge; pull down and lift up.

• Stencil the winter trees in green. Let dry, but leave the stencil in place. Once the green paint dries, dab white paint lightly with a large-holed sponge over each tree for a snowy look. Use the same technique to add touches of spring or fall color to trees and bushes.

• Stencil all windows with a thin coat of white paint first. Allow to dry, then paint over with yellow, blue, or gray.

• Using a sponge with almost-dry green paint, dab some paint above the window boxes to make greenery.

Pen Work

Refer to the drawings below and on page 106, and the photographs on pages 100 and 104.

1. With a wide-tipped black pen, outline all the buildings, windows, doors, trees, icicles, etc.
2. With a narrow-tipped black pen, scribble in the details shown in the line drawing.
3. Referring to the photographs, shade the houses and trees with colored permanent fabric markers as desired, copying the details.
4. Press to heat-set (page 15).

Finishing

Refer to the directions on pages 20–24 to finish your quilt. I hand quilted diagonally across the muslin nine-patch squares and around the buildings. Quilt around any element that you want to "pop" out.

To piece bindings, sew the green print 2" x 6" pieces to 2 of the binding strips to lengthen (top and bottom bindings). Press the seams open.

Sew the binding to the quilt using a ⅜"-wide seam.

Embellishment

1. Choose 4 ribbons for corner trees. Make tacked ribbon bows (page 28) on tops of pine trees and trunks of shade trees.
2. Sew on buttons, charms, and details as desired. Anything relating to a season or holiday is great.
3. Beads are fun to use as lights in your buildings. Look for strings of beads as in the red-green-gold string of lights on the lodge in the winter scene. Couch these strings on at intervals to look like strung lights. Or, make your own string of lights (see the lights connecting the fall buildings). Sew on each bead with a backstitch, leaving a short length of thread between beads like wire between lights.
4. Sign and date your work. Hang your Town Squared quilt and turn it as the seasons change.

Trees

Fence

Pen-work details

105

Clock
(Button)

School

Cottage

Outhouse

Church

Lodge

Small Shutter House

Window Box House

Large Shutter House

Pen-work details

106

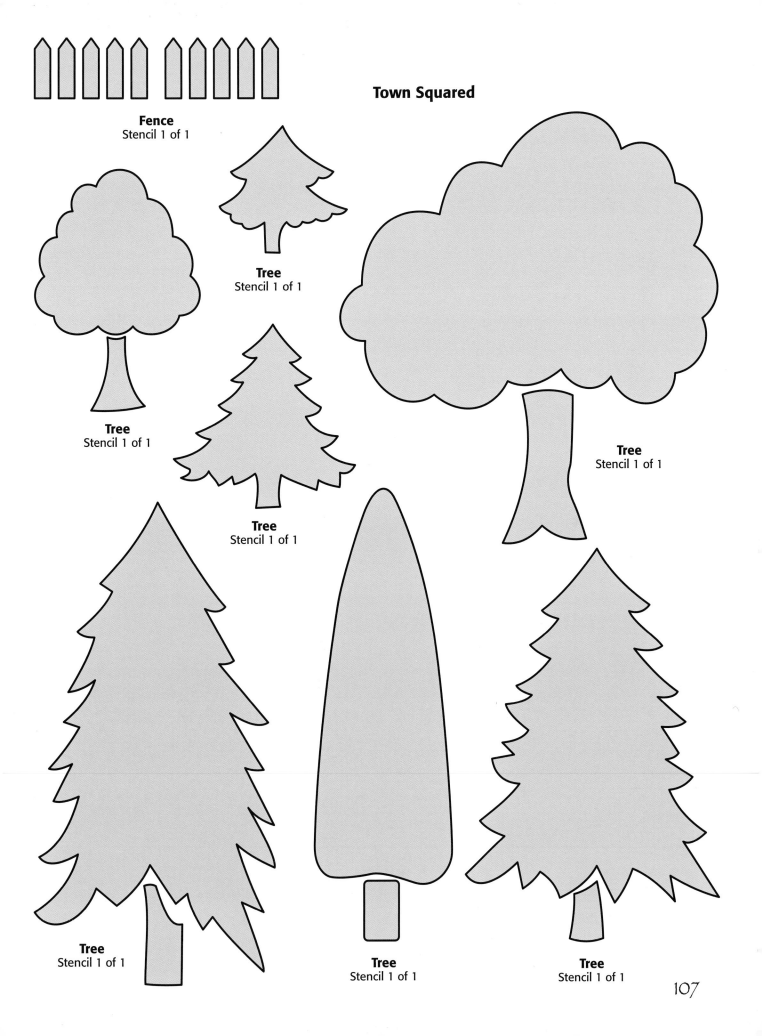

Fence
Stencil 1 of 1

Town Squared

Tree
Stencil 1 of 1

Tree
Stencil 1 of 1

Tree
Stencil 1 of 1

Tree
Stencil 1 of 1

Tree
Stencil 1 of 1

Tree
Stencil 1 of 1

Tree
Stencil 1 of 1

107

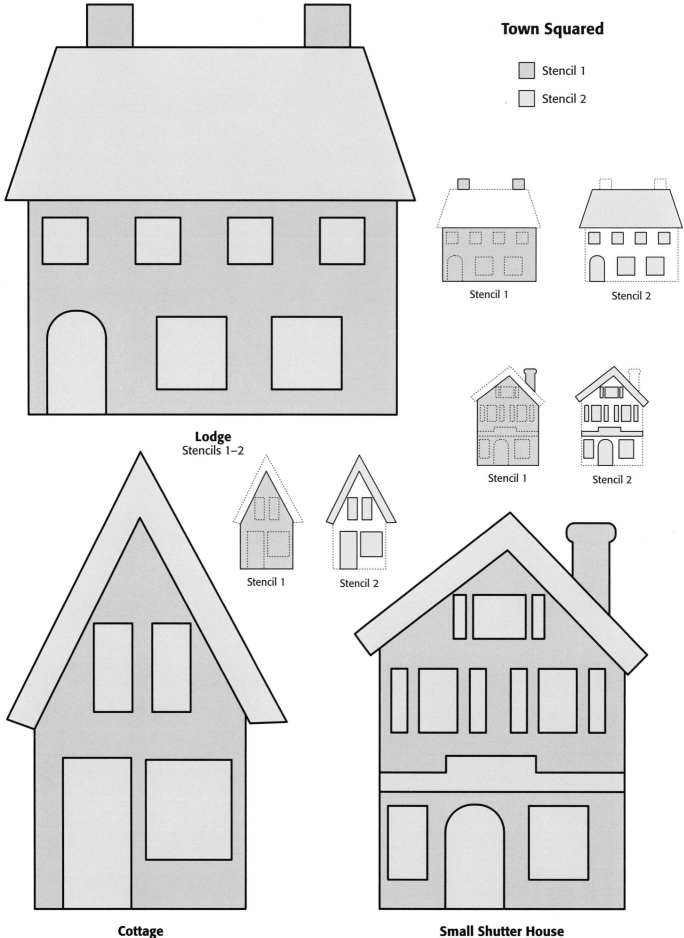

Town Squared

■ Stencil 1
□ Stencil 2

Stencil 1

Stencil 2

Lodge
Stencils 1–2

Stencil 1

Stencil 2

Stencil 1

Stencil 2

Cottage
Stencils 1–2

Small Shutter House
Stencils 1–2

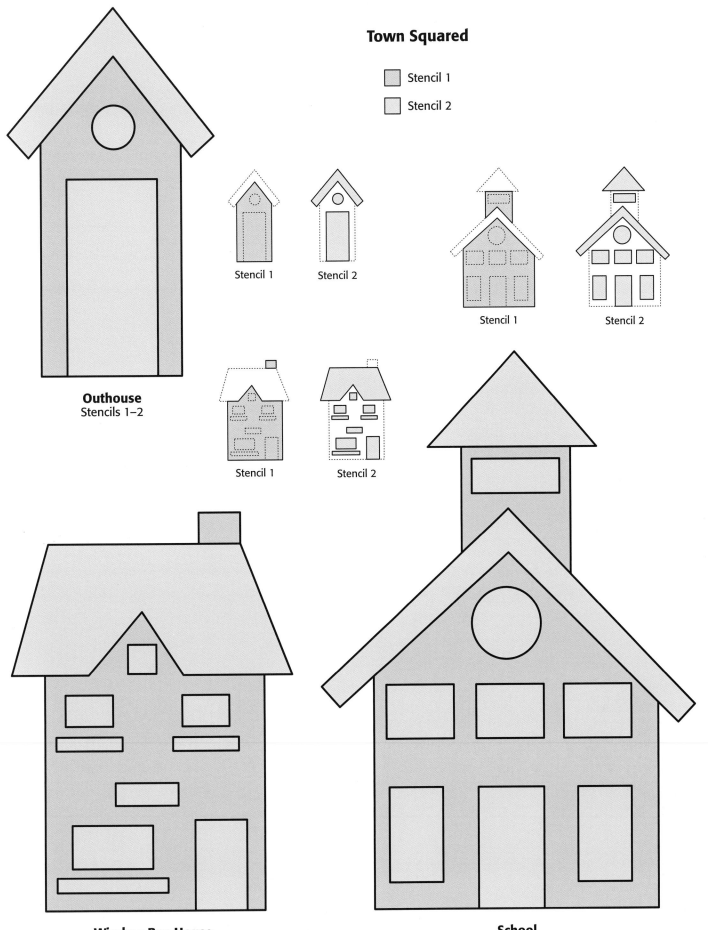

Town Squared

Stencil 1
Stencil 2

Stencil 1   Stencil 2

Stencil 1   Stencil 2

Outhouse
Stencils 1–2

Stencil 1   Stencil 2

Window Box House
Stencils 1–2

School
Stencils 1–2

109

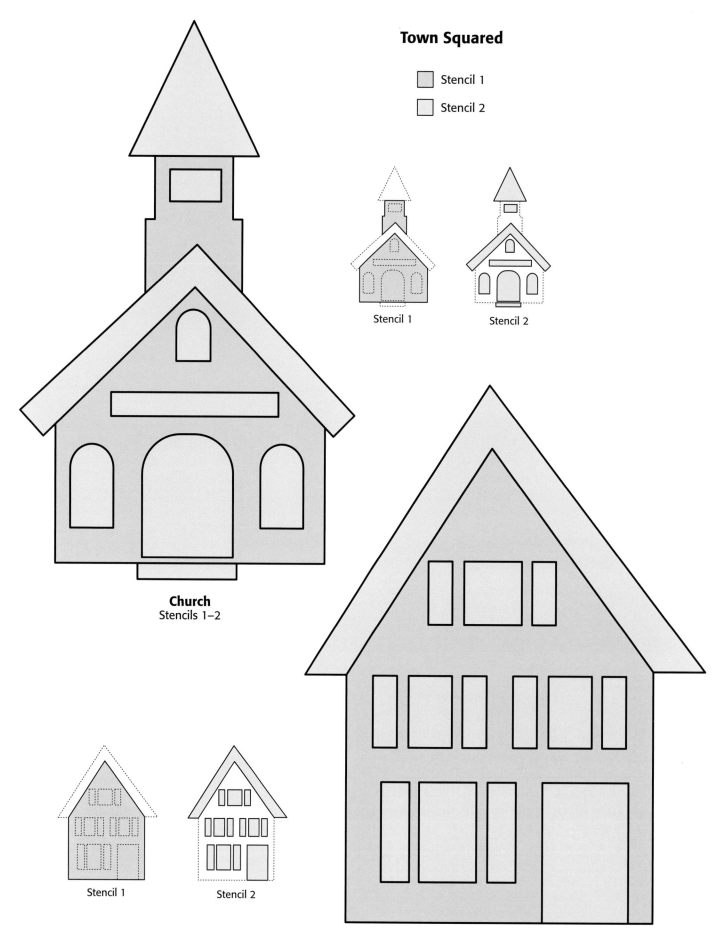

Town Squared

Stencil 1

Stencil 2

Stencil 1

Stencil 2

Church
Stencils 1–2

Stencil 1

Stencil 2

Large Shutter House
Stencils 1–2

About the Author

Vicki Garnas grew up in Bakersfield, California, when it was still a rural oil and farming community. After earning a degree in English from California State University at Northridge, Vicki worked for the Los Angeles Police Department as a civilian station officer for four years, then left police work to raise her family.

Vicki learned how to sew from her mother and how to quilt from books. She began stencil-ing quilts after Marti Sandel shared her patterns and techniques at a quilt-guild meeting. With no formal artistic background, Vicki has developed a simple way to make unusual quilts using common paints, pens, and embellishments. She has taught and lectured extensively throughout Southern California and has demonstrated her techniques on the Carol Duvall Show. Two of her stencil designs have appeared in *American Patchwork and Quilting* magazine.

Books from Martingale & Company

Appliqué
Appliqué in Bloom
Baltimore Bouquets
Basic Quiltmaking Techniques for Hand Appliqué
Basic Quiltmaking Techniques for Machine Appliqué
Coxcomb Quilt
The Easy Art of Appliqué
Folk Art Animals
From a Quilter's Garden
Fun with Sunbonnet Sue
Garden Appliqué
Interlacing Borders
Once Upon a Quilt
Stars in the Garden
Sunbonnet Sue All Through the Year
Welcome to the North Pole

Basic Quiltmaking Techniques
Basic Quiltmaking Techniques for Borders & Bindings
Basic Quiltmaking Techniques for Curved Piecing
Basic Quiltmaking Techniques for Divided Circles
Basic Quiltmaking Techniques for Eight-Pointed Stars
Basic Quiltmaking Techniques for Hand Appliqué
Basic Quiltmaking Techniques for Machine Appliqué
Basic Quiltmaking Techniques for Strip Piecing
Your First Quilt Book (or it should be!)

Crafts
15 Beads
The Art of Handmade Paper and Collage
Christmas Ribbonry
Fabric Mosaics
Folded Fabric Fun
Hand-Stitched Samplers from I Done My Best
The Home Decorator's Stamping Book
Making Memories
A Passion for Ribbonry
Stamp with Style

Design Reference
Color: The Quilter's Guide
Design Essentials: The Quilter's Guide
Design Your Own Quilts
The Nature of Design
QuiltSkills
Surprising Designs from Traditional Quilt Blocks

Foundation/Paper Piecing
Classic Quilts with Precise Foundation Piecing
Crazy but Pieceable
Easy Machine Paper Piecing
Easy Mix & Match Machine Paper Piecing
Easy Paper-Pieced Keepsake Quilts
Easy Paper-Pieced Miniatures
Easy Reversible Vests
Go Wild with Quilts
Go Wild with Quilts—Again!
It's Raining Cats & Dogs
Mariner's Medallion
Paper Piecing the Seasons
A Quilter's Ark
Sewing on the Line
Show Me How to Paper Piece

Home Decorating
Decorate with Quilts & Collections
The Home Decorator's Stamping Book
Living with Little Quilts
Make Room for Quilts
Special-Occasion Table Runners
Stitch & Stencil
Welcome Home: Debbie Mumm
Welcome Home: Kaffe Fassett

Joy of Quilting Series
Borders by Design
The Easy Art of Appliqué
A Fine Finish

Hand-Dyed Fabric Made Easy
Happy Endings
Loving Stitches
Machine Quilting Made Easy
A Perfect Match
Press for Success
Sensational Settings
Shortcuts
The Ultimate Book of Quilt Labels

Knitting
Simply Beautiful Sweaters
Two Sticks and a String
Welcome Home: Kaffe Fassett

Machine Quilting/Sewing
Machine Needlelace
Machine Quilting Made Easy
Machine Quilting with Decorative Threads
Quilting Makes the Quilt
Thread Magic
Threadplay

Miniature/Small Quilts
Celebrate! with Little Quilts
Crazy but Pieceable
Easy Paper-Pieced Miniatures
Fun with Miniature Log Cabin Blocks
Little Quilts All Through the House
Living with Little Quilts
Miniature Baltimore Album Quilts
Small Quilts Made Easy
Small Wonders

Quilting/Finishing Techniques
Borders by Design
The Border Workbook
A Fine Finish
Happy Endings
Interlacing Borders
Loving Stitches
Quilt It!
Quilting Design Sourcebook
Quilting Makes the Quilt
Traditional Quilts with Painless Borders
The Ultimate Book of Quilt Labels

Rotary Cutting/Speed Piecing
101 Fabulous Rotary-Cut Quilts
All-Star Sampler
Around the Block with Judy Hopkins
Bargello Quilts
Basic Quiltmaking Techniques for Strip Piecing
Block by Block
Easy Seasonal Wall Quilts
Easy Star Sampler
Fat Quarter Quilts
The Heirloom Quilt
The Joy of Quilting
More Quilts for Baby
More Strip-Pieced Watercolor Magic
A New Slant on Bargello Quilts
A New Twist on Triangles
Patchwork Pantry
Quilters on the Go
Quilting Up a Storm
Quilts for Baby
Quilts from Aunt Amy
ScrapMania
Simply Scrappy Quilts
Square Dance
Strip-Pieced Watercolor Magic
Stripples Strikes Again!
Strips That Sizzle
Two-Color Quilts

Seasonal Projects
Christmas Ribbonry
Easy Seasonal Wall Quilts

Folded Fabric Fun
Holiday Happenings
Quilted for Christmas
Quilted for Christmas, Book III
Quilted for Christmas, Book IV
A Silk-Ribbon Album
Welcome to the North Pole

Stitchery/Needle Arts
Christmas Ribbonry
Crazy Rags
Hand-Stitched Samplers from I Done My Best
Machine Needlelace
Miniature Baltimore Album Quilts
A Passion for Ribbonry
A Silk-Ribbon Album
Victorian Elegance

Surface Design/Fabric Manipulation
15 Beads
The Art of Handmade Paper and Collage
Complex Cloth
Creative Marbling on Fabric
Dyes & Paints
Hand-Dyed Fabric Made Easy
Jazz It Up

Theme Quilts
The Cat's Meow
Everyday Angels in Extraordinary Quilts
Fabric Collage Quilts
Fabric Mosaics
Folded Fabric Fun
Folk Art Quilts
Honoring the Seasons
It's Raining Cats & Dogs
Life in the Country with Country Threads
Making Memories
More Quilts for Baby
The Nursery Rhyme Quilt
Once Upon a Quilt
Patchwork Pantry
Quilted Landscapes
Quilting Your Memories
Quilts for Baby
Quilts from Nature
Through the Window and Beyond
Two-Color Quilts

Watercolor Quilts
More Strip-Pieced Watercolor Magic
Strip-Pieced Watercolor Magic
Watercolor Impressions
Watercolor Quilts

Wearables
Crazy Rags
Dress Daze
Easy Reversible Vests
Jacket Jazz Encore
Just Like Mommy
Variations in Chenille

3/99